AF172925

Jane Lawson has explored Japan with rare devotion for more than forty years. A former chef, food publisher and respected food and travel writer, she is known for her deep cultural insight and her instinct for drawing out Japan's essence from the details of everyday life.

The author of *Zenbu Zen*, *Yoshoku* and *A Little Taste of Japan*, Jane is also the founder of Zenbu Tours, a boutique travel company offering immersive culinary and cultural experiences, and Zenbu Home, an online store celebrating Japan's handcrafted and timeworn objects.

SECRET
JAPAN

秘密の日本

JANE
LAWSON

affirm
press

affirm press

First published in Australia in 2026 by Affirm Press,
a Simon & Schuster (Australia) Pty Limited company
Wurundjeri Woiwurrung Country
Level 3, 162 Collins Street, Melbourne VIC 3000
Affirm Press is located on the
unceded land of the Wurundjeri Woiwurrung peoples
of the Kulin Nation. Affirm Press pays respect to their
Elders past and present.

New York Amsterdam/Antwerp London Toronto Sydney/
Melbourne New Delhi

Visit our website at
www.simonandschuster.com.au

AFFIRM PRESS and design are trademarks of Affirm
Press Pty Ltd, Inc., used under licence by Simon &
Schuster, LLC.

For more than 100 years, Simon & Schuster has
championed authors and the stories they create. By
respecting the copyright of an author's intellectual
property, you enable Simon & Schuster and the author to
continue publishing exceptional books for years to come.
We thank you for supporting the author's copyright by
purchasing an authorised edition of this book.

No amount of this book may be reproduced or stored
in any format, nor may it be uploaded to any website,
database, language-learning model, or other repository,
retrieval, or artificial intelligence system without express
permission. Inquiries may be directed to Simon &
Schuster, 1230 Avenue of the Americas, New York, NY
10020 or permissions@simonandschuster.com.

All rights reserved, including the right to reproduce this
book or portions thereof in any form whatsoever without
prior permission of the publisher.

10 9 8 7 6 5 4 3 2 1

© Jane Lawson 2026

The moral rights of the author have been asserted.
A Cataloguing-in-Publication entry for this book is
available from the National Library of Australia

9781923046412 (paperback)
9781761822490 (ebook)

Cover design by Daniel New
Front-cover photograph by Sebastian Hages/Unsplash
All other photographs by Jane Lawson
Interior design by Kate Barraclough
Printed and bound in China by
C&C Offset Printing Co., Ltd

MIX
Paper | Supporting
responsible forestry
FSC www.fsc.org **FSC® C008047**

For the wanderers and dreamers – those who have already opened their hearts to Japan's endless wonder and those who soon will.

For the deep thinkers and creators – so often undervalued yet the ones who make beauty tangible.

For all who find grace and meaning in both tradition and change.

Contents

The Way of This Book

During the process of writing *Secret Japan*, I was repeatedly asked, 'What's your new book about?' Whenever I explained that I was hoping to encourage a deeper, more connected way to travel Japan, I'd be shot a quizzical look, and then be tested with, 'But don't you need time for that?'

While an extended exploration of Japan is more ideal than a quick stopover, time is a luxury (as we know), and most travellers can only afford around two weeks away from work, family, pets or other commitments. I wish to help you get the most out of your Japan trip in whatever timeframe is doable for you, even if it's a handful of days – and then to build on it when, and as, you are able. While subsequent Japan trips might sound like a grand assumption on my part, as many of you are about to find out – and plenty of you will have already discovered – it's almost impossible not to return once Japan seeps into your bloodstream. This country has an uncanny knack for getting under your skin.

To let your journey through these pages develop as freely as the travels I hope they inspire, I've refrained from including traditional chapters. Instead, you'll find doorways and laneways through which to wander and ponder, ducking over one bridge of information to the next, in your own time and in whichever direction feels natural, taking breaks as needed to appreciate and process before moving on.

Each doorway or path you choose, and when and how you come to be there, leads to a range of scenarios and possibilities that expose you to a level of understanding of Japan, its culture and people, and a sense of its mysteriously palpable yet intangible energy.

While the personal stories I share on these pages could have taken place almost anywhere in Japan, you may note that I regularly refer to Kyoto. I've spent a large portion of my life in the ancient capital over the decades, having lived there on and off. Kyoto introduced me to my husband in 2011 and provided the launchpad for my tour business, Zenbu Travel, in 2013. Living in Kyoto, I broadened my understanding of Japan after 25 years enthusiastically but somewhat unconsciously 'touristing', wearing rose-coloured glasses for the most part. I consider Kyoto my second home – it's filled with good friends and places and things I adore. However, there are many smaller and undiscovered Kyotos waiting for you, as I've been fortunate to discover – and I'm not just referring to the so-called 'Little Kyotos' noted around the country, like those in Kanazawa in Ishikawa Prefecture, Akizuki in Fukuoka, Shimanto City in Kochi or Tanba-Sasayama in Hyogo. There are many regions that will resonate with you based on a combination of their attributes and your personal interests.

I have not attempted to cover every city and village, nor impart every fascinating glimmer I've gleaned about the culture and the people of Japan – that would be impossible (and ridiculous to try). And trust me – the more I know, the more I realise how much I still have to learn.

I haven't included exhaustive lists of where to go and what to do, because there's already so much of that out there, plus there are endless amazing places to discover on your own.

Instead, I've filled the pages with broader, real-life experiences and observations from over four decades in Japan, sprinkled with some of my favourite places, spaces or experiences – because really, who doesn't love a solid recommendation from a trusted source?

While I've mostly included venues that have stood the test of time, please understand there are no guarantees that things will remain unchanged before you visit. The upside of this is that attempting to locate something that no longer exists may well lead you somewhere better.

I may have included many, many food references. Okay, I definitely did, and I don't apologise for it. Food is not only an important part of the greater Japanese culture, but it features strongly in my life and work, in and outside of Japan.

This isn't a traditional guidebook, but more an inspirational

handbook to dip in and out of. I have included important general information, etiquette and tips – skipping the 'easy-to-find-elsewhere' stuff in favour of lesser-known yet equally helpful practical information.

As you move through these pages, you'll find an enormous collection of suggestions for your time in Japan, some of them quite subtle – Easter eggs, if you like. Some of this information is woven into the text, other bits appear in lists or as boxed information.

Please remember that everything I share in this book aims to provide a starting point for your own discoveries. I believe that you cannot know where to look if you don't know what to look for.

NB: In Japanese romanisation, words are sometimes written with accents over the o or u to indicate that the vowel should be extended – for example, Tōkyō ('Toh-kyoh') or Kyūshū ('Kyoo-shoo'). I've gone with the common practice of omitting the accents throughout this book.

Hajimemashite
– An Essential Introduction

To fully appreciate all that Japan offers as a destination, it's essential not to attempt to do and see it all, not to cram too much into your journey or aim to tick all the boxes – never rush, as tempting as it might be. Wandering without agenda in Japan is terribly underrated.

Strolling Tokyo's quieter backstreets.

With more captivating sights, sounds, experiences and adventures than a human could squeeze into a lifetime – maybe even two – planning a Japan trip can quickly escalate into overwhelm, whether you're a first-time traveller or a devoted returnee.

An enormous amount of misinformation floats unregulated in cyberspace forums. It often comes from instant 'experts' with one-dimensional views based on one or two visits. Additionally, advice, tips and hints online are sometimes 'free' because sponsorship makes them biased.

Equally underwhelming is the restrictive, cookie-cutter rhetoric and guidance found in certain travel guides. Others are on a par with the most antiquated and clunky of Japanese tourism websites. For all Japan's futuristic tech, design and wonder, some things remain stubbornly stuck in a former era. Thankfully, more and more tourism bodies are evolving their online material, with some surpassing expectation. This is a trend that will continue and no doubt supersede the most applauded international sites – because that's how Japan rolls.

Regardless of the difficulties of the information funnel, a constant desire to see it all or keep up with the Joneses may well cause the downfall of any potentially meaningful, authentic experience of Japan.

The term 'authentic' in this instance should not be confused with what many perceive as a 'traditional' Japan experience. For example, I'm not suggesting sleeping every night on futon-topped tatami flooring in a centuries-old ryokan (traditional inn) deep-breathing cedarwood and cypress oils as you slip into slumber via cricket concerto. Nor am I advocating daily kaiseki dining or onsen soaks, visiting every temple, shrine and garden within reach; nor, indeed, mastering the art of straddling a squat toilet when bound in kimono. Even for those still living more traditionally, many of the things we outsiders believe showcases the 'real' Japan are in fact carried out relatively infrequently due to expense, inconvenience or discomfort.

Look around and you'll notice that most Japanese people enjoy the mix of old and new, but certain fragments of the culture are reserved for special occasions, formality or necessity. Tradition is, of course, an important and wonderful part of any Japanese experience, and you should absolutely dive into it – but a more engrossing, truer depiction of Japan comes from a sum of many fascinating parts.

When I speak of authenticity, I'm talking about discovering aspects of Japan travel that occur naturally along the way, or those you are inexplicably drawn to engage with. It's important to remain open to how, why and when these might occur.

Like the country itself, this book is full of texture. My aim in writing it is multifaceted – I want to provide the kind of useful insight you won't find easily elsewhere – that is, what it can look, taste, smell, sound and feel like to truly *be* in Japan – and also to suggest how best to immerse yourself in the culture and better understand it. I hope to help you hear things unspoken, reading visual cues that cannot be seen unless they are explained. I wish to inspire and instil confidence in your travels and assist as you build pathways to discover the best of Japan for yourself – and the best of you, for Japan. To encourage this different way of 'doing' Japan, I've dug deep into the recesses of 40-plus years of Japan travel memories, slowly picking threads woven into the 'I ♥ Japan' blanket I have inadvertently and sometimes purposely sashiko-stitched around my life.

Despite my knowledge and experience of Japan as a frequent explorer, tour guide, travel writer and presenter, it's still sometimes

Fushimi Inari Taisha (shrine), Kyoto. Visit super early to avoid crowds.

challenging to slow down while travelling. I understand it can be tempting to skim across the country's surface like a human pebble, but, from first-hand experience, I can confidently say that this attracts little more than chafing and vertigo. Instead, I encourage you to let your mind and body float through the country's unfathomable layers, soaking up its majesty. I have spent way too long considering how to explain what makes this country so special, and how best to enjoy it. In the end, I took a very deep breath before concluding that the number one thing I recommend doing when travelling Japan is to let go of expectation.

This may be easier said than done.

Expectation can be suffocating, robbing you of life's most rewarding opportunities and circumstances. It is crucial to embrace the Japan that chooses to introduce itself to you, as opposed to the one painstakingly planned for, or the one you hoped would be served on a platter. This concept can be applied to many destinations, but not quite in the same way. On the surface, at least initially, Japan may present as you'd anticipated. However, it does not operate like any other country. I feel qualified to make that call, both as a long-term Japan obsessive and accidental travel writer.

Fascinating opportunities fortuitously manifest when Japan determines you are ready, and this occurs more often and more richly the deeper you go. Japan can feel like a Nintendo game in that you need to attain a certain level of understanding before venturing further – without this understanding, you'll quickly find yourself back at the start, left utterly confused about where you misstepped. Little is straightforward, despite appearances.

Perseverance is very much rewarded in Japanese society, and the more you gently and steadily nudge away, the more this destination unfurls like a lotus flower on a summer's day. Japan's incredible culture reveals itself to you in keesubaikeesu (case-by-case) mode,

and that requires observation, respect, introspection and inevitable return travel.

To describe this country's ancient and modern history and culture as 'complex' would be a gross understatement. However, some relatively recent insight into the shaping of today's Japan comes via the Edo period's (1603–1868) Sakoku (locked country) policy, which restricted entry and exit for over 230 years. This included a shorter, more strict self-isolation bubble that saw Japan completely disconnected from the outside world. This prolonged seclusion helped preserve Japan's deep and unique culture – it was less affected by the ways of the heavily Christian-influenced 'Western world' in which many of us live today.

Several years ago, I quietly took it upon myself to, wherever and whenever possible and appropriate, act as an advocate for the lesser-known Japan. I visited often, channelling my love into areas that deserve and desire visitation. I hope that prompting folks to travel more broadly, at less obvious times and in slightly different ways – even if it is 'just for the blossoms' – will aid decongestion in over-touristed hubs.

If you're in the 'no convincing required, I'm already in love with Japan' camp, then why not venture further by throwing a dart at the map. There's so much nuance to discover – every pocket of Japan carries its own flavour and tempo, which continues to amaze me.

If you've been to Japan recently, think how special it might be to experience it minus the tourist throng – what a gift to yourself and the locals of whichever prefectural pocket you end up in. Exploring a Japanese village that's frozen in a former era can feel like extracting exquisite bounty from a time capsule. Your visit can quickly turn into 'news of the day' in the inaka (countryside), attracting curious new friends and finds. Imagine helping to reinvigorate a town's life force by respectfully sharing its unique characteristics with fellow travellers, before immersing yourself in another equally deserving corner of the country and conveying its marvels. Repeating this practice rewards everyone.

I encourage you to consider Japan as a sentient being, allowing it to approach you in the same way you might reassure a cautious bird that it's safe to take food from your hand. Ground yourself, breathe, stay calm and open, and it will respond. I promise. Even on those occasions when it feels like everything's gone a bit wonky.

Just wait, because the beauty will be revealed when you least expect it.

Visit Umaji village's famous yuzu farms with a village elder. Kochi Prefecture, Shikoku.

The Benefits of Wanderlust

Cold air pressed against my lungs as I hiked the narrow access way between the north and south divisions of the Otani Honbyo (cemetery). Square fingers of concrete jutted out like a small city of high-rise apartments for the dead; the skies were evocatively bleak and ominous. Perhaps there'd be snow? I'd hauled my body up this incline on many occasions – inexplicably, it comforted me. Looking back over the incredible sprawling vista from the top of the hill, which led to Kiyomizu-dera's outer gardens, felt like validation. I'd also shared the scene with my father on his only visit to Japan, not long before his sudden death.

Kyoto's Otani Honbyo is located just south of Kiyomizu-dera (temple).

On this occasion, I noticed people en masse as they scrubbed with frenzy around the vestibules cradling the ashes of their loved ones. I witnessed the replacement of desiccated petals with fresh blooms, the lighting of votive candles and incense, the pouring of sake into ochoko. Others carefully placed the deceased's favourite chocolate bar or fruit. I watched them pray and bow deeply before taking leave with their buckets and every skerrick of detritus. I was mesmerised, but having observed the extraordinary ballet for an obscenely long and intrusive time, I could no longer feel the tip of my nose. It was time to go.

Walking home through town, I noticed shopkeepers airing, sweeping and polishing their premises. Closer to my apartment, the same treatment was being applied to homes.

My laptop informed me that this process of deep cleansing (osoji) for the year's final day (omisoka) is primarily done to purify the venue to welcome the kami (deity) of the new year (o-shogatsu). It's also a nifty way of symbolically clearing any emotional debris from the year that's been, for entering the oncoming 12 months with a clean slate. Once properties are purified, shimekazari – sacred Shinto ropes decorated with lucky ornaments – are hung in doorways to drive away evil spirits, and kadomatsu (decorations of fresh bamboo, pine and sometimes plum stem) are placed either side of gates or doorways, welcoming Toshigami-sama (diety/ies of new year), who temporarily reside in a home's tokonoma (interior alcove). This display is accompanied by an offering of Kagami mochi (large, dried rounds of pounded sticky rice, crowned with a bitter orange). Infused with godly powers, the mochi are traditionally broken into small pieces on 11 January, grilled until molten and popularly served in zenzai (sweet red bean soup). In most homes, this symbolises the release of health and prosperity blessings issued by the Toshigami, as well as their departure.

At the height of my captivation, I scoured my abode from top to bottom, then bought ingredients for making both toshikoshi soba (year-crossing noodles, typically eaten before midnight) and ozoni for New Year's Day (a time of resting and enjoying symbolic foods with family).

I arranged fresh flowers in the tokonoma, lit my favourite incense and tealights, then lathered and showered myself clean before soaking in the bath. Which I scrubbed again. Alone, I watched the red and white *Kohaku Uta Gassen* (musical concert), which has aired on NHK (Japan's public broadcaster) TV since 1953. I ate my noodles around 11pm and, from the stroke of midnight, I reflected over Joya no Kane (the pealing of a Buddhist temple bell 108 times, popularly believed to ward off evil by banishing 108 worldly temptations and sins), as they echoed through the cool night air.

The following year, I joined a newly acquired friend at a neighbourhood temple where we sipped warm medicinal sake with spices (illness-preventative otoso), toasted our gloved hands by drum

fires and mingled with locals. When the time came, I climbed the stairs to the enormous bell's platform and took a deep breath before swinging a tree-on-a-rope into its side with all my might and silently set intentions for the new year. The reverberations through my body were intense, anchoring me to the moment, until I was politely persuaded to make way for those next in line.

With the year officially closed at midnight, hatsumode (the all-important first shrine visit of the year) becomes imminent. Strolling through the lightest snow from temple to shrine, to sip sweet, warm amazake (a low- to no-alcohol cloudy rice drink) and purchase omamori, omikuji and ema (lucky amulets/fortune slips/wooden prayer plaques) is a fun and lovely thing to share. One year at the Yasaka Shrine I purchased rope wick, one end lit by a sacred bonfire of purifying herbs, and spun it all the way home to keep it alight. I transferred its flame to a 'protective-red' candle in my home and gazed into its force until the sweetest sleep beckoned.

Islands Apart
– Japan's Eclectic Regions in a Dragon-shaped Nutshell

No matter what region you visit in Japan, from major city to tiny village, remote island to formidable mountain range, you'll write your own travel story every time. Each experience varies from the next and is always uniquely yours, with its own personalised gifts. Regardless of the scenario, differences in local culture, landscapes, personality and energy – not to mention the opportunities for learning and mind expansion – are endless. Even within a short radius, things can shift dramatically.

The grounds of Shisen-do (temple) are stunning year-round, Kyoto.

Of course, deciding where to start or what to include in your journey can be difficult when you are spoiled for choice. Below, you'll find a pared-back map of Japan, which instantly informs of the country's eight regions (regularly stated as nine for tourism purposes, separating the odd coupling of Kyushu and Okinawa) and the prefectures within them (which run from number 1 in the north to number 47 in the south). Some larger regions are divided into subregions; for example, Chubu subdivides into Hokuriku (north-west) – you'll know the name if you've taken the Hokuriku shinkansen – Koshin'etsu (north-east), and Tokai (south), which each contain several of the regions' prefectures. Other regions even mix prefectures from across neighbouring regions, but to include them here would unnecessarily complicate things.

Breaking Japan down into manageable bites and spending quality time within a certain proximity saves time, energy and money. It also develops a deeper understanding and appreciation for not only the area, but also for greater Japan. Jumping between a wide range of destinations, merely eyeballing each, is unsatisfying, taxing and significantly increases your environmental footprint.

What I'm inviting you to view as 'mood boards' offer an overview of highlights from each region and prefecture – a diving platform from which to initiate your own investigation, going as deep as you wish, adding and subtracting from your personalised mood board as desired, finding threads from which to weave your own bespoke itineraries.

Japan really is so densely packed with allure. It would be impossible – despite its petite stature (similar to Germany in size, fitting 26 times into a map of the United States and 20 times into Australia) – to experience it all.

Regions and Prefectures of Japan

Hokkaido

1. Hokkaido

Tohoku

2. Aomori
3. Iwate
4. Miyagi
5. Akita
6. Yamagata
7. Fukushima

Kanto

8. Ibaraki
9. Tochigi
10. Gunma
11. Saitama
12. Chiba
13. Tokyo
14. Kanagawa

Chubu

15. Niigata
16. Toyama
17. Ishikawa
18. Fukui
19. Yamanashi
20. Nagano
21. Gifu
22. Shizuoka
23. Aichi

Kansai

24. Mie
25. Shiga
26. Kyoto
27. Osaka
28. Hyogo
29. Nara
30. Wakayama

Chugoku

31. Tottori
32. Shimane
33. Okayama
34. Hiroshima
35. Yamaguchi

Shikoku

36. Tokushima
37. Kagawa
38. Ehime
39. Kochi

Kyushu & Okinawa

40. Fukuoka
41. Saga
42. Nagasaki
43. Kumamoto
44. Oita
45. Miyazaki
46. Kagoshima
47. Okinawa

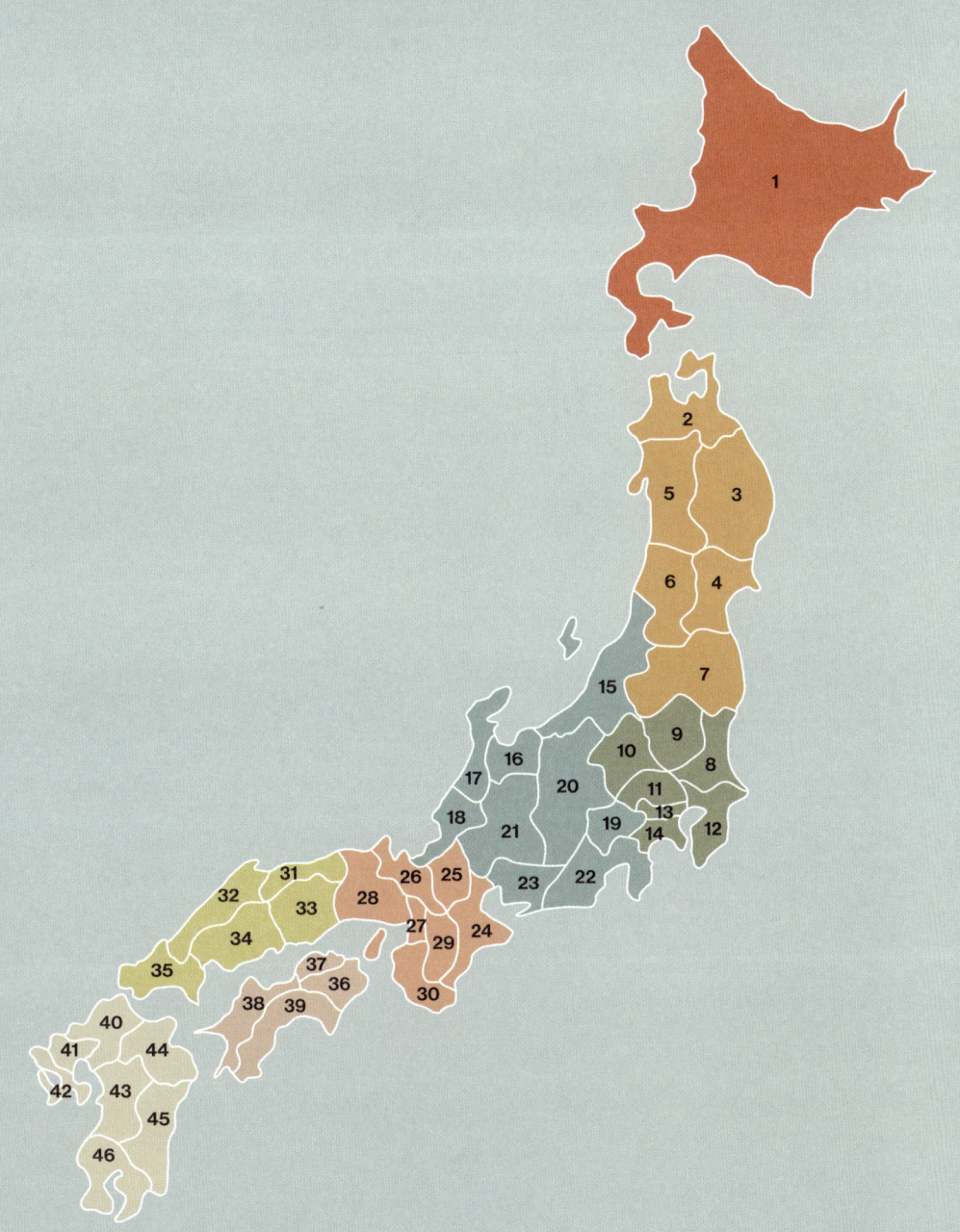

The Big Five
– An Overview of Japan's Islands

Japan consists of thousands of islands, many of them uninhabited, but most foreigners will only recognise the main five. From largest to smallest, they are Honshu (central), Hokkaido (north), Kyushu (south-west), Shikoku (south-east) and Okinawa (further south). I can't help but see the shape of a dragon in their collective make-up, possibly crossed with a seahorse? Tell me I'm wrong.

Above: Kyoto city's quieter northern fringe.
Below: Colourful homes en route to Hokkaido's Otaru.

Zooming out for a moment, a sweeping perspective of the islands might look like this:

Honshu offers a chocolate box of major cities and cultural centres, with all that accompanies each. From dense residential expanses and industrial hubs to blissful holiday spots, Honshu's situation includes both heavily forested mountains and seaside resorts. From dynamic, economically forward cities to the sleepiest pockets, Honshu offers an eclectic platter of microcultures. A small handful of well-documented destinations within the region are where most tourists focus their time. However, there's so much more to discover within short distances of each, and the diversity between destinations is astounding.

Hokkaido, a region and prefecture in one, has a single major city (Sapporo) and several interesting smaller townships. It boasts a vast expanse of natural landscape, panoramically set for summertime hiking, forest bathing, cycling and adventure (good for self-driven scenic escapades too), but better known for winter, when incredible mountains drenched in powder (or, as the kids say, 'Japow') are buzzing with ski and snow play. Indigenous Ainu culture sits quietly at its heart, deserving of more focus, while fireside scenes spark imagination and artistry. Hokkaido's people can seem more reserved than those from Honshu, but often share a similar weariness over peak tourism and ignorant foreigners. Rich in agriculture and fisheries, with famous ports hauling in uber-fresh seafoods to stock their vibrant markets, dining is a priority; locals are mad for ramen and dairy-centric sweets, fine boozy beverages and effervescent izakaya scenes.

Kyushu's people can at first seem delightfully old-school, but they are super genki – proud and genuinely interested in what you are experiencing, why you're visiting and how you view their region. Being so close to southernmost Korea, the people of

Kyushu are perhaps a little bolder and more approachable than some other regions. Even their cuisine is punchier (see p. 216). A pretty posy of cities and towns anchor the region's sublimely green and rolling prefectures. These are dotted with creative cultural villages and farming lands offering everything from cosmopolitan coffee scenes to peace parks and coveted onsen escapes. Famous fishing ports and markets and the odd canal town boast excellent seafood and blissful vistas. This is an easy region to self-drive or shinkansen-hop from top to bottom, and a haven for cycling enthusiasts.

Shikoku is particularly laid-back, especially in the more remote and rustic Kochi Prefecture along the eastern coast, separated from the busier west by dividing ranges. Shikoku locals love their island, which is happily distanced from the mainland – despite being a short train, car or boat ride across the Seto Naikai (Seto Inland Sea). Independent attitudes have persevered throughout this time-warping island, having remained separate from Honshu until a suspension bridge was constructed in 1985. Locals are nonplussed about you being there – everyone's welcome – particularly in Kochi, where folks eat, drink and party with unrivalled merriment. Blanketed with roller-coaster mountains and deep valley villages, earthed in farmland and forest, and famed for autumn scenery (and goat-track roads), Shikoku is also fringed by fishing ports, surf beaches and terraced citrus groves.

Okinawa's stunning islands are super chill, floating in an aquamarine clear soup edged by white sand beaches with incredible scuba and snorkelling spots. It's also graced with jaw-dropping coastlines, rustic villages and lush green spaces. Sometimes referred to as 'the Hawaii of Japan', Okinawa is a popular holiday

Above: Kochi's sunshine-drenched mountain farms, Shikoku.
Below: Nagasaki City's Megane (spectacles) Bridge, Kyushu.

destination for the Japanese. Inhabitants operate on island time, swaying and hopping to their own rhythms (sometimes fuelled by awamori and snake wine), and it can take a minute to slip into the flow when travelling from fast-paced cities. Locals enthusiastically demonstrate the former Ryukyu Kingdom's unique hospitality, culture and medicinal plants, but they are reluctant to discuss the US military presence – which is fortunately quite easy to avoid, as bases are relatively contained. Self-driving makes discovery of the larger of these stunning islands highly convenient. Okinawa's main island is 2.5 hours' drive from top to bottom, boasting exotic Michi-no-Eki (see p. 216) en route, while Ishigaki Island takes one hour from tip to toe.

Small islands scattered throughout the country are assigned to

Micro marine organisms form star-shaped sand on Kaiji beach, Taketomi Island, Okinawa.

the nearest prefecture yet retain autonomous character traits. The less manufactured or commercial – 'do and see' – stuff on offer, the more natural and native your discovery is likely to be.

Good starting points for diving into island microcultures include the many islands within the **Seto Inland Sea** surrounded by the prefectures of Hyogo, Okayama, Hiroshima, Yamaguchi, Ehime, Kagawa and Tokushima, which offer camping, beaching, relaxation and exploring. This inland sea is also the location of the famous 'Seto Art Islands'. Just off Tokyo Prefecture's east coast you'll find the **Izu Islands** (also accessible from Shizuoka Prefecture's stunning Izu Peninsula) – a cluster of volcanic islets with white sandy bays and coral reefs. Further south-east are Tokyo's more remote and sleepy **Ogasawara Islands**. The rustic **Goto Islands** (all 140 of them), whose gorgeous beaches recline off Nagasaki Prefecture, display their historic Christian and Chinese influences. And the World Heritage Site **Yakushima Island**, below Kagoshima, offers a barely touched, biodiverse landscape of primeval forests, ancient ravines and sea turtle colonies. Blissful **Sado Island** in the Sea of Japan, west of Niigata, is the sixth-largest of Japan's islands and is known for its sake breweries, rich food culture and breathtaking landscapes. Shimane Prefecture's windswept **Oki Islands**, a UNESCO Global Geopark, are fringed with fishing villages and brushed with pastural plateaus. Legend suggests they were the third islands formed when sibling Shinto gods Izanagi and Izanami created the Japanese archipelago, with Nu-jima (Nu Island, originally mythical Onogoro) in southern Awaji-shima the first island, and Shikoku (see p. 128) the second. From Izanagi's left eye, the sun goddess Amaterasu (see p. 156) was born – the divine ancestor from whom the Imperial line is believed to have descended.

Let's zoom in a little closer now to look at the regions and prefectures.

REGION 1.

Hokkaido
(1 prefecture)

Hokkaido
(No. 1 – Total cities: 35)

Japan's northern frontier feels a world apart – big skies, dramatic coastlines, and a food culture shaped by pristine seas and fertile plains. Winters shimmer with snow festivals and steaming onsen escapes, while summer brings flower fields and sweet alpine air. Sapporo blends lively nightlife with modern creativity; Otaru charms with canal-side nostalgia; and the wilderness calls from Shiretoko to the high peaks of Daisetsuzan. Come hungry for crab, scallops, dairy and a sense of space you won't find elsewhere in Japan.

Above: Bird's eye view of Hakodate's fortified Goryokaku.
Below: Otaru's excellent Kaisendon (seafood bowls).

CITIES, TOWNS & VILLAGES

Sapporo (**capital**) – vibrant food culture; atmospheric Susukino precinct nightlife; ramen and izakaya yokocho (alleys); Sapporo Snow Festival; Sapporo Beer Museum; the late-night sweets ritual of shime parfait; easy access to Jozankei Onsen (where seasonal shrine rites and first-fruits customs echo ancient nature beliefs); young designer enclaves; subterranean shopping.

Hakodate – historic international port with Western influences; red-brick warehouse (shop/dine) district; atmospheric Motomachi Slope; Fort Goryokaku; lively Asaichi Morning Market full of seafood (crab tanks, squid fishing); cosy cafe scene; hillside night view among Japan's top three.

Asahikawa – second largest city; snow and ice festival; gateway to several ski resorts, such as those in the Daisetsuzan mountain range; close to Biei/ Furano villages; izakaya-hopping; woodcraft and indigo dyeing; ramen village (rich oily shoyu broth); Heiwa-dori pedestrian (shop/dine) street; Ainu culture.

Otaru – romantic canal lined with stone warehouses, now busy with cafes, galleries and daytrippers; sweet and dessert shops along the main strip; rustic seafood market with superb kaisendon.

Obihiro – Tokachi's farming hub; famous butadon (grilled pork bowls); dairy-rich sweets; unique ban'ei horse racing with draft horses pulling sleds; lively farmers' markets.

Kushiro – foggy port town; birthplace of robatayaki charcoal-grill dining; Washo Market with kattedon (build-your-own) seafood bowls; gateway to wetlands and crane sanctuaries (cranes locally revered as long-life messengers).

Muroran – steel and port heritage; striking coastal cliffs; wild sea views.

Abashiri – Okhotsk coastal hub; winter drift-ice tours; ship and sea myths; frontier history anchored by the Abashiri Prison Museum.

Wakkanai – Japan's northernmost city; edge-of-Japan lore; ferries to Rishiri and Rebun islands; lighthouse viewpoints; windswept capes.

Furano and Biei (neighbours, often visited together) – panoramic drives through rolling farmland; patchwork hills, lavender fields, flower gardens; skiing; artisanal cheese, jam, ice cream, wine; creative farm-to-table stays.

Niseko – world-renowned powder snow; cosmopolitan 'united' villages; farm restaurants rooted in local produce; craft breweries.

Akan-ko – a sacred lake with marimo moss balls carrying protective lore; epic songs keep spirits close; Ainu Kotan village with nightly dance and storytelling; rustic lakeside onsen ryokan.

Toyako Onsen village (**Lake Toya**) in Toya-Usu UNESCO Global Geopark – caldera lake; fireworks over the water; Showa-shinzan volcanic dome, Mount Usu ropeway views.

Jozankei – historic hot spring town of soothing waters, stunning scenery and mythical water sprites (Kappa) in a forested valley near Sapporo.

Esashi – historic herring boom town; preserved merchant houses; fisher-folk song (Esashi Oiwake) and sea omen traditions.

Mombetsu – drift-ice viewing centre; fishing culture; port town atmosphere.

Shibetsu – salmon hometown; salmon ecology museum; seasonal salmon festivals.

Above: Hokkaido Jingu, Sapporo.
Below: Fisherman's shrine torii gate at Otaru's Nishin Goten (Herring museum).

OUTLYING ISLANDS

Rishiri – volcanic cone of dormant Rishiri-'Fuji' mountain in Rebun-Sarobetsu National Park; alpine wildflowers; circumnavigation cycling; Rishiri kombu; ferries from Wakkanai.

Rebun – 'Flower Island' with highland trails above sheer coasts; Cape Sukoton and Cape Gorota; small fishing hamlets; pairs naturally with Rishiri, on the same ferry line.

Okushiri – remote Sea of Japan isle off Hiyama; sea cliffs and the Nabetsuru-iwa rock arch; quiet beaches; sweet, plump seasonal uni; a poignant 1993 tsunami memorial; ferries from Esashi/Setana; flights from Hakodate.

Teuri – seabird sanctuary with sunset cliffs and guided colony viewing; ferry from Haboro (Rumoi coast).

Yagishiri – pastoral sister to Teuri: gentle forest walks and coastal lanes; low-key island life; same ferry route as Teuri.

TEMPLES, SHRINES & GARDENS

Hokkaido Jingu (shrine) (Sapporo) – spiritual heart in Maruyama Park; plum and cherry blossoms; New Year visits.

Kamikawa Shrine (Asahikawa) – guardian of the mountains; site for observance of seasonal rites.

Ubagami Daijingu (Esashi) – one of Hokkaido's oldest shrines, prayers for fishing hauls and harvests.

Botanic Gardens (Sapporo) – alpine flora; preserved Ainu houses; ethnographic displays (plants/animals framed as spirited beings).

HISTORIC PRECINCTS

Hakodate Motomachi – Nineteenth-century hillside international quarter; Western-style consulates, houses; Catholic and Russian Orthodox churches; Kanemori red brick warehouses – legacies of port trade.

Otaru Canal & Sakaimachi Street – merchant district; stone warehouses; eateries; sweet, dairy-rich souvenirs.

Esashi herring mansions – reminders of the boom years when herring fuelled Hokkaido's wealth.

MUSEUMS, GALLERIES & CULTURAL LIFE

Abashiri Prison Museum (Abashiri) – open-air historic site; recollections of frontier development and convict labour; ghost tales still told on winter nights.

Historical Village of Hokkaido (Sapporo) – open-air museum; frontier life in action.

Asahiyama Zoo (Asahikawa) – penguin parades and natural habitat enclosures for behavioural observations.

Sapporo Art Park (Geijutsu no Mori) – expansive outdoor sculpture garden, rotating exhibits.

Moerenuma Park (Sapporo) – Isamu Noguchi-designed landscape art park; glass pyramid; sculptural landforms.

Hokkaido Museum of Modern Art (Sapporo) – regionally significant contemporary artworks, international collections, serene garden setting.

Ainu Kotan (Lake Akan) – indigenous cultural theatre; crafts; storytelling (Yukar oral literarture, poetry and spirit-invoking dance).

Okhotsk Ryu-hyo Museum (Mombetsu) – displays and films; drift-ice science; frozen-room experience.

Nibutani Ainu Culture Museum (Biratori) – Ainu cultural celebration; masterful woodcarvings; textiles; living traditions.

Upopoy National Ainu Museum & Park (Shiraoi) – interactive open-air centre for traditional Ainu culture and ongoing revitalisation.

Asahikawa Design Center (Asahikawa) – contemporary wood furniture and craft showcase.

TRADITIONAL CRAFTS & EXPERIENCES

Kita no Arashiyama (Asahikawa) – artisan village; furniture and woodworking ateliers; indigo dyeing and pottery studios.

Ainu workshops in embroidery, woodcarving, and traditional instrument (mukkuri) – motifs reference owls, bears and protective patterns.

Kamiiso washi – Hokkaido natural fibre paper; workshops are available.

Above: The slopes of Hakodate's historic Motomomachi precinct.
Below: Asahikawa's izakaya laneways.

FESTIVALS & PERFORMANCE

Spring

Various flower festivals – Sakura at Fort Goryokaku (Hakodate) and Matsumae Park (Matsumae). Ume (plum) at Hiraoka Park (Sapporo). Fragrant lilac ('tree of Sapporo') at Odori and Kawashimo Parks (Sapporo). Shikisai-no-oka flower fields (Biei, from late April).

Mashike's Shrimp and Harvest festivals (May) – honouring local delicacies.

Summer

Yosakoi Soran Festival (June, Sapporo) – high-energy street dance.

Hakodate Port Festival (August) – squid dance, drums and chanting.

Wakkanai Northern Festival – life at Japan's edge marked with dances and fireworks.

Togyo Festival (August, Ubagami Shrine, Esashi) – spirit-transporting parades; elaborate mikoshi (portable shrines).

Farm Tomita (Furano, July) – fragrant lavender fields.

Autumn

Esashi Oiwake Festival (September) – folk-singing competitions for old seafaring melodies.

Hokkaido's seafood markets are a true highlight for foodies.

Sapporo Autumn Fest (September and October) – open-air gourmet harvest in Odori Park.

Akan Lake Marimo Festival (October) – torchlit procession; conservation conversations.

Winter

Sapporo Snow Festival and Asahikawa Winter Festival (February) – colossal snow and ice sculptures; fireworks.

Lake Shikotsu Ice Festival (January and February) – illuminated frozen creations.

Otaru Snow Light Path (February) – canals and backstreets light up with lanterns.

FOOD & DRINK

Ramen – a perfect base for self-guided ramen pilgrimages – Sapporo miso (often topped with butter and corn); Asahikawa shoyu (soy and/or miso-based); Hakodate shio (clear, salt-based, clean and briny); Muroran kare (curry broth, chewy, curly noodles).

Soup curry – richly spiced broth with chicken, meat or seafood and seasonal vegetables, sometimes cream or cheese; workshops available.

Ishikari nabe – nourishing salmon and miso hotpot native to the Ishikari River region.

Obihiro butadon – Tokachi's signature sweet–savoury pork rice bowls.

Jingisukan – lamb barbecued on convex grills; shaped like Genghis Khan's hat.

Seafood – hairy, king and snow crab; uni (sea urchin); ikura (roe); scallops; kaisendon (seafood bowls) – combinations of above over warm rice; Akkeshi oysters; hokke (grilled atka mackerel) – an izakaya staple.

Markets – Sapporo Nijo Market; Hakodate Morning Market; Kushiro Washo Market; Otaru Sankaku Market (hello, kaisendon!).

Farm produce – Tokachi potatoes; Furano and Yubari melons; sweet corn; asparagus; mushrooms; fruit picking; Furano jam; cheese-making and ice-cream classes.

Sansai – mountain vegetables and herbs; guided foraging and cooking classes in eastern Hokkaido.

Dairy and sweets – soft-serve ice cream; milk; butter; cheeses; cheesecake and tarts; ROYCE' Chocolate; Shiroi Koibito biscuits; Marusei butter sandwiches; shu-kuriimu (cream puff).

Drinks – Sapporo Beer Museum and breweries; Nikka Whisky Yoichi Distillery; crisp cold-climate sake; new-wave craft beers and cider; tastings and brewing tours; summer festival beer gardens.

NATURAL HIGHLIGHTS

Daisetsuzan National Park – volcanic ranges; wildflowers; autumn foliage; alpine onsens filled with the mountain spirits that figure in Ainu cosmology.

Sounkyo Gorge – dramatic cliffs, waterfalls, restorative alpine onsen in Daisetsuzan National Park.

Shiretoko Peninsula – a frontier where the divide between human and spirit realms feels thin; UNESCO World Heritage Site; waterfalls; wildlife; drift ice cruises; brown bears, sea eagles, foxes; remote fishing hamlets at the 'edge of the earth'; Ainu reverence for Kimun-Kamuy (the mountain bear) emphasises the 'wild' in 'wilderness'.

Kushiro Marshlands – red-crowned cranes (revered auspicious messengers); canoeing; boardwalks.

Cape Soya (Wakkanai) – Japan's northernmost tip, dramatic windswept landscape facing Sakhalin (Russia).

Biei (Blue Pond) – surreal cobalt waters, submerged skeletal larch trees.

Noboribetsu Onsen & Jigokudani (Hell Valley) – steaming 'demon breath' volcanic vents; sulphur springs.

Unkai Terrace (Tomamu) – suspended observatory for dawn 'sea of clouds' phenomena.

Flower fields of Furano – lavender; sunflowers; wildflowers in summer.

Lake Mashu – deep volcanic caldera lake; ethereal fog; too-clear views foretell of change.

Rishiri and Rebun – alpine blooms; island hiking and cycling; views of conical Rishiri-fuji.

Above: Fisherfolk brave Otaru's craggy coastline.
Below: Moerenuma Park's gentle slopes.

REGION 2.

Tohoku
(6 prefectures: Aomori, Iwate, Miyagi, Akita, Yamagata, Fukushima)

Aomori
(No. 2 – Total cities: 10)

At Honshu's northernmost fringe, soulful Aomori shares a kinship with neighbouring Hokkaido – both are shaped by heavy winters and a fierce closeness to nature. Snowbound months yield to orchards dense with apple blossoms, spring trails reappear through mountains and gorges, and summer nights burst with the colour of Nebuta's illuminated lantern giants. The outdoors link fishing harbours, ski fields, cedar forests and hot-spring hamlets, anchoring life through each season. Art and invention surface in cider houses and contemporary museums, and lacquer and embroidery traditions are patiently honed through long winters.

Above: Towada Art Centre.
Below: Nebuta Museum Wa Rasse.

CITIES, TOWNS & VILLAGES

Aomori City (capital) – port city; Nebuta Museum Wa Rasse; A-FACTORY cider and apple-centric goodies; Furukawa Fish Market nokkedon (build-your-own bowls); Aomori Prefectural Museum; access to Asamushi Onsen.

Hirosaki – castle town famed for cherry blossoms, best in Hirosaki Castle Park; Tsugaru cultural traditions; Niji-no mart (local market); apple orchards; small cafes, shops and galleries in kura (storehouses).

Hachinohe – lively port city with excellent morning markets; Hasshoku Center food hall; Tatehana wharf; fishing town atmosphere; Kabushima Shrine stands at the coast.

Towada – gateway to Lake Towada and Oirase Gorge; Towada Art Center blends nature and cutting-edge contemporary art.

Goshogawara – known for Tachineputa Festival, with towering floats paraded through the streets; once home to literary master Osamu Dazai; nostalgic stove train cuts through snow plains.

Kuroishi – hot-spring town; centre of Tsugaru lacquerware; nearby Nuruyu Onsen's rustic baths; Komise Street's covered arcade; old onsen lanes.

Shimokita Peninsula – remote; Osorezan (Mount Osore) temple complex; fishing villages and Cape Oma (tuna capital); Yagen Gorge and Onsen as a quiet forest base.

Hirakawa – Seibien historic building and garden; Araya colour-changing onsen; Tsugaru clan traditions and crafts, e.g. Kokeshi dolls, Neputa floats.

Mutsu – base town for exploring the Shimokita Peninsula; samurai history; wild coastlines.

Tsugaru – west coast city facing Sea of Japan; access to Shirakami-Sanchi ancient forest trailheads; windswept dunes of Shayo-misaki cape, Fukaura/Senjojiki coast.

TEMPLES, SHRINES & GARDENS

Osorezan (Mount Osore, Shimokita) – pilgrimage site tied to the afterlife; sulphuric landscapes; spiritual traditions.

Seibien Garden (Hirakawa) – traditional strolling garden; both Japanese and Western elements.

Hirosaki Castle Park (Hirosaki) – iconic cherry blossoms; moats; historic turrets.

Kabushima Shrine (Hachinohe) – seaside shrine dedicated to the black-tailed gulls who bring the shrine to life.

Seiryu-ji (Aomori) – the Showa Daibutsu; one of Japan's largest seated Buddhas.

Iwakiyama Shrine (Mount Iwaki) – grand cedar approach at the Tsugaru 'Fuji'.

Fujita Memorial Garden (Hirosaki) – villa and strolling garden; castle-town aesthetics.

HISTORIC PRECINCTS

Hirosaki Castle town – Edo-period samurai houses and kura; cherry-blossom-filled moats.

Tatehana Wharf Morning Markets (Hachinohe) – unstaged; rooted in local life; still essential for fishermen and locals.

Kuroishi onsen streets – rustic hot-spring town; cobbled laneways; historic baths; attractive Komise Street (Edo-period covered arcades protected from the elements).

Sannai-Maruyama Jomon Site (Aomori) – vast prehistoric settlement; reconstructed pit dwellings and longhouses.

Hirosaki's local market and castle grounds.

MUSEUMS, GALLERIES & CULTURAL LIFE

Nebuta Museum Wa Rasse (Aomori City) – festival floats; wondrous craftsmanship.

Towada Art Center (Towada) – contemporary art in dialogue with the landscape.

Tachineputa Museum (Goshogawara) – home to giant parade float exhibits.

Aomori Museum of Art – modern architecture by Jun Aoki; Chagall's Aleko theatre backdrop; Yoshitomo Nara's whimsical work.

Hirosaki Apple Park – orchards; apple history; tastings.

Osamu Dazai Memorials (Goshogawara) – celebrating the local-born author's life and works in the palatial Shayokan building.

Local cider houses and indie cafes – emerging creative culture; stunning kura spaces.

Hirosaki Museum of Contemporary Art (MOCA) – red-brick cider brewery reborn as a space for site-specific contemporary art.

Hachinohe Portal Museum/'hacchi' – community art hub; markets; design events.

Sannai-Maruyama Jomon Museum – rare tools, fibres and hints of everyday life from 5000 to 4000 years ago.

Inakadate rice paddy art (tanbo art) – field-scale images in living rice; viewed from towers (June to October; peak mid-summer).

Tsugaru Railway Stove Train – winter cars with coal stoves; squid grilling; a rolling slice of culture.

TRADITIONAL CRAFTS & EXPERIENCES

Tsugaru traditional craft centre (Kuroishi) – regional handicraft museum.

Tsugaru-nuri lacquerware (Kuroishi/Hirosaki) – bold, mottled lacquer styles; studio visits; small workshops.

Tsugaru shamisen – distinctive, percussive shamisen music; lessons or intimate local performances available.

Tsugaru vidro (glass) – softly coloured hand-blown glass; factory shop; demos around Aomori.

Kogin-sashi embroidery – white-on-indigo (traditionally) geometric stitching; born of winter necessity; studio classes.

Apple harvest and cider-making – orchard visits; tastings; seasonal hands-on experiences; pie trails.

Nebuta craft – paint a Kingyo (goldfish) Nebuta; try washi/glue work on float panels.

FESTIVALS & PERFORMANCES

Summer

Aomori Nebuta Festival (early August) – towering illuminated floats; drumming; dancing.

Hirosaki Neputa Matsuri (August) – painted fan-shaped floats; distinct from Aomori City's Nebuta.

Goshogawara Tachineputa (August) – enormous hand-crafted floats reaching around 23 metres tall.

Hachinohe Sansha Taisai (late July to early August) – floats; mikoshi; neighbourhood community focus.

Towada Summer Festival (August) – bands; food lanes; lake breezes.

Inakadate rice paddy art (June to October) – breathtaking giant field-canvas, best viewed in peak summer.

Autumn

Hirosaki Castle Chrysanthemum and Autumn Foliage Festival (late October to November) – maples; 'mums'; castle walls.

Takko Garlic Festival (October) – Aomori's famed garlic; grilled and celebrated.

Shirakami beech hikes – clear days; golden canopy; Anmon Falls in season.

Winter

Hachinohe Enburi Festival (February) – farmers dance for a good harvest through snowy streets.

Views of Hirosaki township from the castle grounds.

Hirosaki Castle Snow Lantern Festival (**February**) – snow Kamakura (igloo); lantern-strewn streets; light projections on walls.

Winter rice paddy art (**Tsugaru**) – textures and patterns, light and shadow.

Spring

Hirosaki Cherry Blossom Festival (**late April to early May**) – castle moat filled with petals, sprawling garden grounds.

Apple Blossom Festival – michno-eki/roadside station Namioka.

Apple blossom drives and walks – around Hirosaki and Hirakawa orchards.

FOOD & DRINK

Apples and cider – defining produce; central to sweets, drinks and culture.

Miso curry milk ramen (**Aomori City**) – a quirky local twist on ramen.

Senbei-jiru (**Hachinohe**) – soy broth hotpot with wheat senbei (crackers) instead of noodles.

Maguro/Oma tuna (**Shimokita**) – revered bluefin tuna variety sold at auctions, eateries and festivals; Shimokita area is renowned for seasonal pole and line catches.

Sake – clean, crisp regional brews; shaped by snowmelt waters; Denshu and Mutsu Hassen brands.

Seafood – scallops, squid and mackerel are central to coastal towns; ichigo-ni (urchin & abalone soup, Pacific coast); kaiyaki miso (Mutsu Bay scallop shell grilled with egg and miso).

Towada Barayaki – beef and onions sizzling on iron with sweet–savoury sauce.

Markets – Hasshoku Center (Hachinohe); Tatehana Wharf Morning Market (one of Japan's largest).

NATURAL HIGHLIGHTS

Lake Towada & Oirase Gorge – autumn colours; hiking; boating; Towadako Ski Resort; snow-shoeing.

Shirakami-Sanchi (**UNESCO World Heritage Site**) – primeval beech forests; trekking.

Hakkoda Mountains – popular ski resorts, walking trails; famous for 'snow monsters' (juhyo or sculptural frosted trees) in winter.

Various hot spring resorts with regional bathing and dining traditions at rustic inns – Asamushi Onsen (Aomori City); Sukayu Onsen with deep snow baths; Nuruyu and Itadome Onsen (rustic 400-year history); Owani Onsen (quiet ski resort area).

Cape Oma – northern tip of Honshu; tuna culture; windswept coasts.

Hachinohe coastline – Tanesashi Coast; wildflowers; surf.

Hotokegaura (**Shimokita**) – otherworldly sea stacks; green water; boat access in season; cliff path views.

Cape Tappi (**Sotogahama**) – windswept strait views; lighthouse lookouts.

Senjojiki Coast (**Fukaura**) – wave-cut stone plateaus; sunset lines.

Mount Iwaki – Tsugaru Fuji, viewed over orchards; Iwaki ski resort; hiking; hill drives.

Asamushi Onsen & Mutsu Bay – bayside baths; small islands; evening boats.

Scenic islets: Yunoshima (Asamushi) and Benten-jima (Fukaura coast).

Above: Everyday scenes in Japan's largest apple-producing region.
Below: Squid grilled inside the Tsugaru Railway Stove Train during winter.

Iwate (No. 3 – Total cities: 14)

Rugged, rural and wild, Iwate's mountains, temples and coastlines are shaped by resilience. Its spiritual heart lies in Hiraizumi, where Pure Land Buddhist gardens and golden halls whisper of paradise on earth. Along the Sanriku Coast, fishing villages carry both bounty and hardship, their tenacity matched by camaraderie. Inland, Wanko soba is slurped bowl after bowl in playful competition, Nambu ironware is still forged with care and festivals fill the streets with taiko drums, horse bells and lantern light. Austere in landscape yet warmly human in spirit, Iwate reveals itself in intimate moments: a jazz record spinning in a smoky cafe; a farmhouse table laid with pickles and sake; the hush of waves folding against the cliffs.

Miyagi (No. 4 – Total cities: 14)

Miyagi moves with quiet confidence. Flamboyant daimyo Date Masamune's legacy still shapes Sendai's avenues and culture. Matsushima Bay's pine-clad islets unfold like a living screen. Naruko Onsen lies in a steep valley ringed by gorges, wooded paths and villages where kokeshi are still carved and painted by hand. Fox lore lingers on Mount Zao's slopes. Miyagi is grounded in tradition but also dynamic and creative: from Ishinomaki's playful manga street and design hubs to Kesennuma's working fish market eateries; from Shiroishi's samurai quarter to Shiogama's sake brewers and Kokubuncho's nightlife.

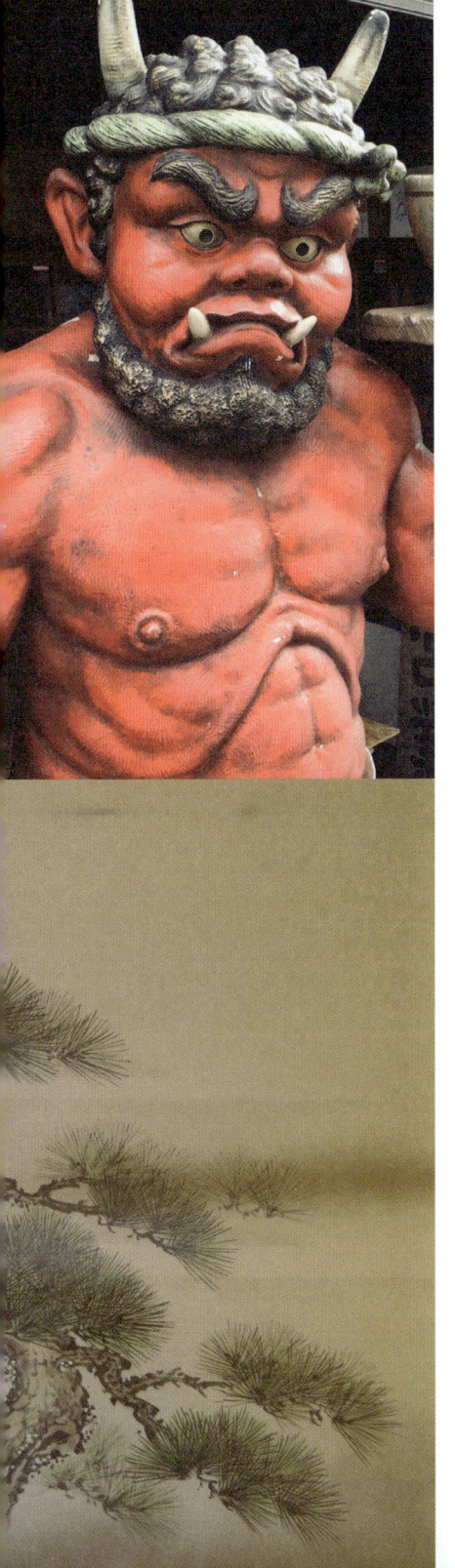

Akita (No. 5 – Total cities: 13)

Relatively wild compared with its more urbanised neighbours, Akita leans into snowbound winters, horizon-wide rice fields and closely held traditions – cedar craft, fermentation, preserving and the samurai artistry of handsome Kakunodate. Community, ingenuity and onsen hospitality define local life. Market gatherings fuel conversation, and cafes hum with students and creatives. Kanto Matsuri's tall lantern poles rhythmically tilt and sway across summer skies, while families huddle around kiritanpo nabe for warmth in winter in anticipation of New Year's Eve when Namahage demons stomp through doorways. From the temples of Mount Taihei to Oga's coastal fishing towns, from deep forests to Yokote's sake breweries, Akita feels seasoned and proud.

Demons and pine artfully reflecting the faces of deep mountain and coastal Tohoku.

Yamagata (No. 6 – Total cities: 13)

Farming and faith entwine in Yamagata. The sacred peaks of Dewa Sanzan draw pilgrims whispering to spirits on meditative treks, while Yamadera's thousand steps echo Basho's verse and mountain trials of Shugendo lore ... Riverside Imoni (beef, taro and soy hotpot), simmered in Yamagata's own cast-iron nabe, honour water guardians who bless the harvest. Shirataka's safflower fields and crimson dye ward off misfortune. Orchards blush with cherries and pears in season while Ginzan Onsen glows like a snow-demon trail each winter. Life centres around asa-ichi (morning markets) brimming with fruit and pickles, kura reimagined as art spaces, and smoky yokocho where stories spill into the night.

Fukushima (No. 7 – Total cities: 13)

Fukushima has a quiet fullness to it. Peaches pile high on roadside tables, sake ages in dark kura and the scent of shoyu ramen wafts through Kitakata's atmospheric alleys. In Aizu castle town, samurai spirit endures – in its brilliant autumn scenery, Tajima Gion festival, Aizu-nuri (lacquer ware) workshops and the thatched roof Edo-era post town of Ouchijuku. Gulls soar across the salty Sanriku coastline seeking seafood market bounty. Michi-no-Eki feel like neighbourhood living rooms, places to pause and talk, not just to buy. Moss-carpeted temples soften into silence and reflection, while Goshikinuma's five coloured lakes shimmer otherworldly hues.

REGION 3.

Kanto
(7 prefectures:
Ibaraki, Tochigi,
Gunma, Saitama,
Chiba, Tokyo,
Kanagawa)

Ibaraki (No. 8 – Total cities: 32)

Often called Tokyo's kitchen garden, Ibaraki is abundant with fertile plains, seafood drawn from rugged coasts, and storehouses packed with natto, miso and shoyu. The waterfalls and flower fields of Hitachinaka redraw the horizon each season. Shrines rise from the surf line at Oarai. Silk looms clatter in Yuki workshops. Mito balances the refinement of Kairakuen (one of Japan's great daimyo gardens) with the energy of its backstreets, which are lined with retro shotengai, coffee roasters, bars, izakaya and an alternative music scene. Innovation flows without limit, from Kasama's lively pottery studios to Tsukuba's 'Science City' research centres. Folks are pragmatic, innovative and open-hearted.

Tochigi (No. 9 – Total cities: 14)

Around two hours north of Tokyo, Tochigi blends spiritual grandeur with craft and community. Tosho-gu, gleaming with gold and enshrining shogun Tokugawa Ieyasu, crowns Nikko's cedar-lined paths. Tochigi is grounded by Mashiko's pottery and indigo dyeing, Kanuma's kumiko timber latticework, Nikko's natural-ice farms and Utsunomiya's gyoza counters. The Nasu highlands blend rich dairy country, sake breweries and family-friendly ski resorts. Satoyama (mountain village) valleys are dotted with kominka (farmhouses) and markets brimming with pickles, mushrooms and Tochiotome strawberries. Irohazaka's hairpin bends climb to Lake Chuzenji, surrounded by onsen ryokan and hiking trails humming with birdsong.

Mount Nantai and blissful Lake Chuzenji in Nikko National Park's highlands.

Gunma (No. 10 – Total cities: 12)

Mountain-ringed Gunma's enduring Jomojin (local people) live in a landscape moulded by volcanic heat and alpine air. Ritual sustains life in Kusatsu Onsen's Yubatake hot-water field, rhythmically stirred and slapped with paddles to calm volatile spirits. The onsen of Ikaho, Minakami and Manza also enjoy loyal followings. Byakue Dai-Kannon towers protectively over Takasaki's Shorinzan Daruma temple – birthplace of the Daruma talisman. In Tomioka, Usui-yaki pottery still fires near the UNESCO World Heritage–listed Tomioka Silk Mill, which remembers the steadfast women who once worked its looms. Food is simple but bold – miso-glazed manju, sweet-roasted Shimonita onions and apples pressed to cider at roadside stalls.

Above: Preserved merchant streets of Kawagoe in Saitama.
Below: Daruma are a symbol of perseverance throughout Japan.

Saitama (No. 11 – Total cities: 40)

Tokyo's northern neighbour, Saitama blends commuter bustle, tradition and surprising natural pockets. In Kawagoe, kura-zukuri merchant streets preserve the atmosphere of old Edo, while Chichibu's Shrine and Night Festivals, Nagatoro's river gorge and Omiya's bonsai village reveal a greener, more contemplative side. Indigo vats bubble in backstreets, Gyoda's tabi are still stitched at kitchen tables and festival floats rumble by on autumn and winter evenings. Saitama's character is unshowy but textured, with community and craft holding fast against the sprawl.

Chiba (No. 12 – Total cities: 37)

Tokyo's salt-licked backyard, enterprising Chiba asserts itself between airport runways and commuter suburbs. Beyond them lie fishing ports and terraced paddies, saw-tooth cliffs and shrine fires. Narita's temple town greets arrivals, while soy sauce brews in Noda and art jostles with industry at Nokogiriyama. Out on the Boso Peninsula, Pacific surf towns face Kujukuri's endless beach, Katsuura simmers chilli-red Tantanmen ramen, and flower fields brighten Tateyama's capes. Chiba is, all at once, gateway, garden and getaway.

Tokyo
(No. 13 – Total cities: 26)

A backdrop to the world's largest metropolis, Tokyo Prefecture relaxes westward into cedar forests, river gorges and mountain onsen, and reaches east to islands scattered in the Pacific Ocean. Within its borders you can move from neon wards and sushi counters to quiet hamlets and subtropical seas – extremes held together under the same name.

Observing Shibuya's famous crossing from above.

CITIES, TOWNS & VILLAGES

Tokyo City (capital)

Tokyo (historically, Edo) promises the best of the best – world-class food, shopping, art and nightlife – yet its essence lies in the rituals of daily life. Edo's shrines and gardens still anchor neighbourhoods where glass towers rise, and yakitori sizzles in under-track alleyways. Tokyo dazzles with scale but draws you in with intimacy, offering both energy and respite, tradition and reinvention. Nowhere else in Japan feels this visceral and exciting.

Tokyo and surrounds – Districts & anchors, as they radiate out from the central core

Central core

Tokyo Imperial Palace – East Gardens and surrounds; short walk from Tokyo Station.

Tokyo Station, Marunouchi (west) and **Yaesu** (east) – primary shinkansen and transport hub; historic red-brick station sits over a subterranean city of tracks; shopping and dining arcades; lifestyle and fashion emporiums like KITTE with its information centre, post office, shops, dining and cafes.

Akasaka – commuter hub; shopping; izakaya and Kaiseki dining precincts; Toyokawa Inari shrine annex.

Ginza – flagship fashion window dressings; excellent shopping (Ginza Six, Itoya); upmarket tea and coffee houses; restaurants and cafes; Kabuki-za theatre; people-watching.

Nihonbashi – Edo's merchant core; historic shops, many in modern quarters; handcrafted foods, fans, incense, brushes, lacquerware and woodblock prints.

Yurakucho and Shinbashi – Smoky gado-shita (under tracks) yakitori alleys; salaryman sightings; commuter Tokyo at its most authentic.

North of central

Kanda, Jinbocho and Ochanomizu – stylish shopping and dining precinct called mAAch ecute Kanda Manseibashi underneath a railway; book town; guitar street; curry joints; second-hand shops; university cafes.

Akihabara – electronics and otaku culture; collectible figurines and maid cafes; Chabara (wide-ranging Japanese foodstuffs); 2k540 Aki-Oka Artisan design precinct.

Ueno – sprawling park with classic museums; Ameyoko market bustle; shinkansen gateway to Northern Japan.

Yanesen (Yanaka/Sendagi/Nezu) – handsome old temple town alleys and cemetery; Yanaka Ginza shotengai, often swarming with tourists; cool cafes and pocket galleries; Nezu shrine's vermillion torii tunnel and azalea blooms.

Nippori – fabric district with retro charm beloved by crafters.

North-west

Kagurazaka – cobblestone alleys; French community; pocket galleries and contemporary Akagi-jinja shrine by architect Kengo Kuma; former samurai precinct with still-operating geisha houses.

Shin Okubo – Tokyo's K-town with yakiniku-filled lanes, Korean skincare, dessert cafes, K-pop merch.

Shinjuku – skyscrapers; department stores; Kabukicho nightlife; Shinjuku Gyoen garden.

Ikebukuro – large station with a shopping and dining complex; Pokémon Center; Otome Road for female manga and anime fans; ramen hub; Chinatown; grassroots makers' markets; small theatres.

Sugamo – oldschool vibes; Jizo Dori shopping strip; obaachan's Harajuku.

Izakaya under train tracks and historic pockets tucked between skyscrapers.

Nakano – Nakano Broadway for anime and manga; rare toys; shopping and dining arcades.

Koenji – vintage fashion; punk and underground music clubs; basement live houses; izakaya clusters.

Kichijoji and Mitaka – Inokashira Park; indie cafes; relaxed vibe; stylish shopping stretches; Harmonica Yokocho's tiny bars and eateries; Ghibli Museum.

Tachikawa – sprawling Showa Kinen Park; eco-minded Green-springs lifestyle complex.

East of central

Fukagawa and Monzen-Nakacho – Kiyosumi Gardens; coffee roaster enclave; Tomioka Hachiman flea markets; canal-side izakaya alleys. Nearby Sunamo ginza (oldschool shotengai).

Tsukishima and Tsukuda – neighbouring riverside islets; Tsukishima for monjayaki (Tokyo okonomiyaki); tiny Tsukuda for tsukudani (seafood, seaweed and vegetables simmered in soy, once preserved on boats).

North-east

Ryogoku and Sumida – sumo stables (some with viewable morning training); Kokugikan Arena; Edo-Tokyo Museum; Sumida Hokusai Museum, Tokyo Skytree, craft breweries.

Kuramae and Torigoe – artists' studios; design store precinct for leather, textiles, bamboo, ceramics, incense, chocolate and homewares; cool cafes; the time-warped shopping strip of Okazu Yokocho.

Asakusa – Senso-ji Temple; Nakamise shopping street; Sumida River cruises; Kappabashi is popular with keen cooks for kitchenware, knives, faux food models.

South of central

Roppongi and Azabudai Hills – international dining; major art facilities including the National Art Center and teamLab Borderless; Mori Art Musuem, Roppongi Hills observation deck and Tokyo Midtown's sleek mix of boutiques, design shops and food.

Azabu Juban – upmarket inner-city pocket with neighbourhood vibe; shopping;

dining and cafes; cool cocktail bars like Gen Yamamoto, Tokyo Confidential, The Lively.

Tennozu Isle and Bayfront – reclaimed waterfront warehouses-turned-cafes, galleries and studios; Terrada Art Complex; WHAT Museum; T.Y. HARBOR brewery; street art; the wondrous colours of PIGMENT TOKYO, a favourite for art and crafters; bay cruises.

Shinagawa – modern station hub housing Tokaido Shinkansen stop; blossom-lined riverside dining strips; Oi Racecourse flea and antique markets; Sengaku-ji (temple – resting place and museum for the famed 47 ronin).

Haneda – modern, convenient international and domestic airport.

South-west

Harajuku, Omotesando and Aoyama – a mixed precinct linking quirky, youth-driven fashions and food to upscale lifestyle boutiques and dining; Meiji Jingu shrine; Yoyogi Park markets and events; sleek design cafes; architecture; patisseries; galleries; Nezu museum.

Shibuya – 'the' crossing; plentiful shopping; Shibuya Sky observations; Miyashita Park; live houses; izakaya; late-night energy; bold design experiments such as the Tokyo Toilet project, where world-class architects rethink the most ordinary urban rituals.

Daikanyama – fabulous T-Site bookstore; indie boutiques; lifestyle shops; dining,

drinking and cafe precinct; Log Road; Kyu-asakura villa/garden.

Ebisu – yokocho; rustic izakaya; cool bars; Tokyo Photographic Art Museum; Yebisu Brewery's beer museum.

Nakameguro – sakura-flanked canal walks; indie boutiques; eateries.

Meguro – parasite museum; antiques street; coffee roasters.

Tomigaya – backstreet cafes and bakeries near Yoyogi Park; relaxed neighbourhood vibe.

Yoyogi-Uehara – residential calm; stylish cafes; craft and design stores.

Shimokitazawa (**Shimokita**) – eclectic; record stores; vintage shops; indie theatre; live bars; izakaya; homewares; coffee roasters; curry festival; weekends lure chilled crowds. Adjacent to bohemian 'slow Tokyo' neighbourhoods of Setagaya-Daita and Ikenoue.

Sangenjaya (**Sancha**) – boho pocket; live music; commuter hub; relaxed local dining scene; Sankaku Chitai's maze of alleyway bars and eateries; nearby Gotoku-ji's maneki-neko origins.

Jiyugaoka (**Jiyuga**) – relaxed but chic; shopping, dining, cafes and patisseries; leafy neighbourhood vibe; popular with mums and bubs who lunch.

Above: Hip Shimokitazawa.
Below: Higashi Nihonbashi neighbours Ryogoku (AKA sumo-central).

South-east

Odaiba Toyosu – tourist-leaning, but fun for young families, artificial islands of malls and arcades; futuristic tech, media and robotic attractions and museums; Toyosu Fishmarkets and Team Lab Planets.

OUTLYING ISLANDS

The **Izu Islands** are a chain of volcanic islands south of the city, each with a different character:

Oshima – closest to Tokyo; Mount Mihara volcano hikes; camellias; coastal onsen.

Toshima – explore by foot only, camellia forest hikes, wild dolphins.

Niijima – surf beaches; laid-back island life; glass and pottery craft.

Kozushima – white sand beaches; snorkelling; quiet fishing hamlets.

Miyakejima – dramatic active volcanic landscapes; birdwatching; hot springs.

Hachijojima – subtropical climate; diving; hiking; remote island culture; kusaya fermented fish; island shochu.

Ogasawara (**Bonin Islands**) – remote UNESCO World Heritage-listed archipelago 1000 kilometres into the Pacific; accessible only by a 24-hour ferry from Tokyo.

Chichijima – tropical; beaches; hiking; whale and dolphin watching.

Hahajima – very quiet; endemic flora and fauna.

TEMPLES, SHRINES & GARDENS

Senso-ji (**Asakusa**) – Tokyo's most famous temple; incense; markets; festivals; long shopping arcades.

Meiji Jingu (**Harajuku**) – giant tori; culturally significant shrine; gardens; Shinto wedding processions.

Zojo-ji (**Minato City**) – historic temple; skyline backdrop.

Nezu Shrine (**Bunkyo**) – torii tunnel; Azalea Festival.

Kanda Myojin (**Chiyoda**) – shrine of techies and anime fans.

Hie Shrine (**Nagatacho**) – dedicated to guardian deity of Tokyo; red torii-lined stairways.

Oiwa Shrine (**Yotsuya**) – linked to Japan's most famous ghost story, Yotsuya Kaidan.

Zenkoku-ji (**Kagurazaka**) – nicknamed Bishamonten by locals; Setsubun rituals with geisha.

Yanaka temple – Tennoji, Kaneiji; Yanaka cemetery; Yanaka Ginza shotengai.

Gotokuji (**Setagaya**) – temple with thousands of maneki-neko (beckoning cat) figurines.

Classic landscaped Japanese gardens – Rikugien; Koishikawa Korakuen; Kiyosumi Teien; Shinjuku Gyoen; Imperial Palace East National Gardens; Kyu Shiba Rikyu; Hamarikyu, Happoen; Nezu museum garden; Mukojima-Hyakkaen; Kyu Asakura House; Kyu-Furukawa; Mejiro Garden; Tonogayato.

HISTORIC PRECINCTS

Yanesen – three-neighbourhood cluster of temples; cemetery; handsome old streetscapes.

Asakusa – shitamachi (oldschool downtown); backstreets vibe; geisha.

Kagurazaka – slope; old samurai precinct; geisha; galleries, Zenkoku-ji.

Shibamata – retro shotengai; riverside Edo and Showa period nostalgia.

Kanda and Jinbocho – old publishing heart, where Meiji era academia met post-war boho.

Sunamachi – daily life centred around rustic but thriving Sunamachi Ginza shotengai.

Ryogoku – sumo stables; river heritage – old bridges, boat moorings and warehouses recall Edo's commercial gateway.

Tsukuda – old town's weathered wooden homes and laneways; Sumiyoshi shrine guarding fishermen; Tsukudani origins.

MUSEUMS, GALLERIES & CULTURAL LIFE

Tokyo National Museum (**Ueno Park**) – 1800s-built institution with impressive national treasures.

Nezu Museum (**Aoyama**) – ancient Japanese and East Asian art, stunning stroll garden.

Mori Art Museum (**Roppongi**) – contemporary art with a view.

Suntory Museum of Art (**Roppongi**) – refined, traditional arts and crafts.

Museum of Contemporary Art Tokyo (**MOT**) (**Koto**) – bold, extensive collection surrounded by greenspace.

Mingeikan (**Meguro**) – Japanese folk crafts museum in handsome old home.

Team Lab (**various locations**) – Borderless (Azabudai Hills); Planets (Toyosu) – deeply immersive light, sound, colour digital art.

Ad Museum Tokyo (**Shiodome**) – advertising reframed as mirror to society.

Sumida Hokusai Museum (**Ryogoku**) – Hokusai's famous prints and sketches.

Edo-Tokyo Museum (**Ryogoku**) – largescale, from samurai capital to modern day.

Shitamachi Museum (**Ueno**) – recreations of Edo period life.

Kyu-Asakura House (**Daikanyama**) – serene 1919-built home and garden.

Yayoi Kusama Museum (**Shinjuku**) – of polkadot and pumpkin fame; immersive, contemporary installations.

Ghibli Museum (**Mitaka**) – for fans of Studio Ghibli animations.

Miraikan (**National Museum of Emerging Science and Innovation, Odaiba**) – interactive exhibits; robots.

Above: Team Lab Planets.
Below: The joyful colours of PIGMENT TOKYO.

Clusters of small indie galleries and museums (Yanasen) – e.g. Asakura Museum of Sculpture, Scai the Bathhouse, Hagiso; similar found in Kagurazaka, Iidabashi, Kuramae, Shimokitazawa and Koenji.

Markets – regular, seasonal or pop-up; flea, antique, handmade/tezukuri, farmers', organic and more; all over Tokyo, including Setagaya Boroichi, Oi Racecourse flea market, Tomioka Hachimangu antique and flea, Tokyo International Forum Antique Fair, Oedo Antique market, Gokokuji Antique Market, Ikebukuro Handmade Market and Ikegami, UNU Farmers' Market, Daikanyama Green Market, Earth Day (slow food) Market.

TRADITIONAL CRAFTS & EXPERIENCES

In more traditional areas like Nihonbashi, Asakusa, Yanesen, Sumida and Fukagawa, Edo traditions endure in fan and brush makers, ukiyo-e print studios, incense, and wagashi stores. Hands-on experiences include calligraphy, tea ceremony, Edo kiriko and furin (cut and etched glass and glass wind chimes), kumihimo (braided silk cords once used in samurai armour and kimono), kimekomi dolls, wood with fabric inlay, indigo, kimono, komon stencil dyeing, sashimono nail-free carpentry techniques. Niijima glass (shaped by volcanic sand) and pottery workshops.

FESTIVALS & PERFORMANCE

Summer
Sanno Matsuri (**June**) – musical processions; courtly pageantry; occurs on even-number years.

Sumidagawa Hanabi (**July**) – spectacular fireworks over Sumida River.

Fukagawa Hachiman Matsuri (**August**) – lively water splashing; Tomioka Shrine.

Autumn
Nezu Shrine Autumn Festival (**September**) – parade; court music; dance; food stalls.

Asakusa Tori-no-Ichi (**November**) – bird day festival at Otori Shrine; lucky rakes; chanting.

Winter

Various – illumination events and Daruma markets (December to January).

Oshogatsu (31 December to 3 January; New Year's eve/day) – Meiji Jingu, Sensooji and Zojo-ji, Hatsumode – first shrine visit of year.

Otakiage (January) – ritual fire-cleansing festival; burn old new-year decorations.

Spring

Sanja Matsuri (May) – Asakusa; big, bustling and intense.

Kanda Matsuri (May) – Edo period mikoshi and floats; occurs on odd-number years.

Cherry blossoms (end March/early April) line the Meguro, Sumida and Zenpukuji Rivers, Chidorigafuchi moat, Ueno, Yoyogi and Asukayama (parks), Shinjuku gyoen, Yanaka cemetery.

Year round

Kabuki (Ginza) traditional stories through dance and song at Kabuki-za theatre.

Noh/Kyogen (various small stages) – meditative, musical drama interjected with short, satirical Kyogen.

Contemporary/subculture performance – various intimate indie theatre and live-houses for jazz/punk/underground music. (Kagurazaka, Shimokitazawa, Kichijoji, Koenji, Shinjuku, Asagaya and beyond.)

Above: Tender Tonkatsu with all the trimmings.
Below: Sushi master at work.

FOOD & DRINK

Tokyo's dining landscape traverses a broad spectrum, from matchbox-proportioned bars and deeply traditional neighbourhood joints to some of the world's most exquisite, contemporary gastro-temples. Tokyo's high-end sushi-ya and fine-dining are among the most exclusive, transcendental culinary experiences on the planet.

Izakaya, yakitori, yakiton (pork skewers) – true after-dark flavour lives under the tracks; smoky gado-shita in Yurakucho, Kanda, Akabane, Akasaka and Koenji; upmarket gado-shita found in cool city pockets; lively izakaya yokocho (laneways) in Shinbashi, Shibuya, Ebisu, Shinjuku, Sengenjaya and beyond.

Ramen – eclectic and cross-pollinated, e.g. tonkotsu-gyokai blends; miso, shoyu, shio and tsukemen styles and contemporary takes. Readily found in train station precincts, e.g. Tokyo and Shinagawa Ramen Streets. Serious clusters in Ikebukuro, Ebisu, Shinjuku, Ueno.

Soba – nutty buckwheat noodles in shoyu (soy) broth, an Edo staple, nourishing 'fast food'.

Tempura – originally a street food found along the docks and markets of Nihonbashi and Asakusa.

Edo-style sushi – born of old Edo; from simple standing bars to universally revered counters.

Chanko-nabe (Ryokaku) and Oden – hearty hotpots, the former protein-rich, designed for Sumo wrestlers; the latter simmered fishcakes, tofu and vegetables found in izakaya (and kombini).

Tsukudani (sweet soy preserved foodstuffs) and Monjayaki (local-style okonomiyaki) – found in neighbouring oldschool precincts Tsukuda and Tsukushima.

Creative dining and kaiseki – Tokyo reinterprets kaiseki traditions with global influences; cutting edge, multi-course, sensory menus (for a few favourites, see p. 216/Gut Instinct).

Patisserie and sweets – glistening pastry and dessert pageantry; everywhere from Ginza to Shibuya to Jiyugaoka; Tokyo also excels at wagashi (yokan, dorayaki, ningyo-yaki).

Kissaten and cafes – from the city to the 'burbs, oldschool kissaten (Ueno, Shinjuku, Jinbocho, Akasaka, shimbashi) balance with design cafes and coffee roasters (Ginza, Aoyama, Yoyogi-Uehara, Kiyosumi Shirakawa, Daikanyama, Nakameguro, Shimokitazawa, Kichijoji, Koenji); contemporary sipping culture with tasting flights, siphon brews and pairing menus; coffee or tea treated with the same reverence as wine.

Depachika – department store basement food halls; Isetan Shinjuku; Nihonbashi Mitsukoshi; Seibu Ikebukuro; several in Shibuya (Scramble, Hikarie)

Tsukiji Outer Markets – crowded but colourful.

Toyosu Fish Market – tuna auctions, though modern and controlled.

Curry culture (Kanda and Shimokitazawa) – spice-scented comfort food enclaves; kare rice; kare pan; katsukare (curry smothered tonkatsu); kare udon.

Oldschool shotengai – daily food shopping; nostalgic neighbourhood vibe; peek into local life; Okazu Yokocho, Sunamachi Ginza, Togoshi Ginza, Sugamo Jizo Dori, Ameyoko (well-known and busy); others in Koenji, Kichijoji, Nakano, Asakusa, Asagaya.

NATURAL HIGHLIGHTS

Meiji Jingu Gaien Ginko Avenue (Aoyama) – autumn ginko trees form a blazing gold, photogenic tunnel.

Todoroki Valley – green gorge; shrines; bamboo groves.

Okutama and Mitake Gorge – rivers; lakes; waterfalls; canoeing; canyoning; hiking; onsen; trails to Mount Mitake's mountaintop shrine; panoramic views.

Mount Takao – Tokyo's beloved hike; cable car access; autumn foliage; temple culture; Mount Fuji views on clear days.

Showa Kinen Park – vast seasonal park of flower fields, ginkgo avenues, cycling routes and boating lakes.

Tamagawa and Arakawa River – riverside walks; weekend cycling.

Izu & Ogasawara Islands – volcanic landscapes; subtropical seas; fishing villages; Tokyo's far frontier (some accessible from the Izu Peninsula, see p. 31).

Above: Tokyo Skytree reaching for the ... (go on, guess).
Below: Mejii Jingu Gaien's golden ginko tunnel.

Kanagawa (No. 14 – Total cities: 19)

Tokyo's neighbour taps a mercurial tempo through its collective port towns, samurai valleys, popular beaches and mountain hot-spring enclaves, all a short beat from the capital. Kanagawa flows from Yokohama's cosmopolitan waterfront through its bustling Chinatown and izakaya laneways towards quieter Kamakura's temple gardens, surf beaches and Fuji-view sunsets before stopping in Hakone's peaceful ryokan and outdoor artscapes. A commuter corridor north to Tokyo on weekdays, and a southern weekend retreat for Tokyo residents seeking coast, temples and onsen calm.

Opposite above: Hasedera, Kamakura.
Opposite below: Kamakura's Daibutsu (great Buddha) at Kotoku-in.
Above: Misty Lake Ashi & Hakone Shrine's torii, Hakone.

REGION 4.

Chubu

(9 prefectures:
Niigata, Toyama,
Ishikawa, Fukui,
Yamanashi,
Nagano, Gifu,
Shizuoka, Aichi)

Niigata (No. 15 – Total cities: 20)

Long, harsh winters have honed life's essentials in Niigata – rice, sake, pickles and salted salmon strung from eaves are revered for their depth of flavour. Patience also shaped enduring crafts: Tsubame–Sanjo blades, snow-bleached textiles and glossy Murakami lacquerware. Nagaoka's fireworks blaze as a symbol of peace in summer, while castle moats glow with spotlit lotuses. In Tokamachi and Yuzawa, snow drifts sculpt into lanterns and figures, and in mountain hamlets art blooms in abandoned fields, proof that resilience seeds renewal. On Sado Island, exile and gold mines left ghost stories and silent Noh stages, spaces now energised by taiko thunder and a thriving food culture.

Toyama (No. 16 – Total cities: 10)

Nestled between the Sea of Japan and the Tateyama peaks, Toyama is a place of extremes. The Tateyama Kurobe Alpine Route cuts through the towering snow walls at Murodo, where frozen waterfalls and crater lakes form natural ice temples. Offshore, Toyama Bay yields white shrimp and firefly squid that glow as much in myth as in catch. In the valleys, UNESCO World Cultural Heritage–listed Gokayama gassho-zukuri farmhouses shelter in heavy snow. Tateyama itself has long been revered as a threshold between worlds, its pilgrim paths edged with awe and caution. Life remains communal: artisans huddle over glass and metal, farmers gather to min'yo ballads, and local markets bustle.

Ski-hop between Niigata and Nagano's shared alpine ranges.

Ishikawa
(No. 17 – Total cities: 11)

Ishikawa stretches like a brushstroke along the Sea of Japan, anchored by Kanazawa – a former castle town shaped by the Maeda clan's patronage of gardens and craft, tapering into the windswept Noto Peninsula to the north and relaxing into Kaga's onsen territory in the south. Kanazawa's appreciation for the finer things endures in Kenroku-en, Kaga-ryori (regional haute cuisine), gold leaf, earthenware and Omicho's bustling seafood market. Noto moves with the elements – neighbours gather at morning markets, salt is coaxed from the tide and festivals erupt with lion dances. Ishikawa beautifully balances both the raw and the refined.

Kanazawa'a charming Higashi-chaya geisha precinct.

CITIES, TOWNS & VILLAGES

Kanazawa (**capital**) – Maeda clan castle town centred around Kanazawa castle and adjacent Kenroku-en garden; flanked by Nagamachi Samurai District and nearby Higashi, Nishi and Kazuemachi Chaya-gai (geisha districts). Highlights include The 21st Century Museum of Contemporary Art; DT Suzuki Museum; lively Omicho Market; the textured Teramachi temple district. Lanes of kura-style coffee houses and flea markets fuel Kanazawa College of Art students and creatives. Galleries and collectives reworking tradition.

Wajima – coastal town of Noto Peninsula known for its 1000-year-plus morning market and lacquerware traditions; Wai Plaza Wajima, where orange-tented vendors temporarily relocated the market's community heartbeat after the 2024 earthquake; Kiriko festivals with giant lantern floats; resilience expressed through craft and community spirit.

Nanao – onsen town of Wakura Onsen, Noto, with long-established inns and sea views; Seihakusai Festival's towering dekayama floats, built by community hands; heritage in the old quarter (some venues under restoration) where the storied Takazawa Candle Shop has handpainted plant-wax candles for over 150 years.

Suzu – the remote tip of the Noto Peninsula; salt fields (Agehama style); Suzu-yaki pottery heritage; strong rustic character; windswept coastlines; a slower pace of life.

Hakui – quirky in character; unofficial UFO capital; Cosmo Isle space and UFO museum; unusual Chirihama Nagisa Driveway, where cars can be driven along the sand beach at sunset; Keta-taisha (shrine) keeps forbidden secrets.

Kaga city – Kaga-Onsen-Kyo (cluster) in forested valleys and the foothills of Mount Hakusan-Yamanaka, Yamashiro, Katayamazu and Awazu Onsens (in neighbouring Komatsu); Kakusenkei gorge; historic Daishoji quarter, Kaga-yuzen dyeing.

Komatsu – gateway city to southern Ishikawa; Kutani porcelain; Yunokuni no mori (craft village).

TEMPLES, SHRINES & GARDENS

Kenroku-en Garden (Kanazawa) – beauty rotates with the seasons; tea houses; ponds; stone lanterns.

Nomura-ke Samurai Residence Garden (Nagamachi) – elegant Edo-era home; intimate, carefully composed garden.

Gyokusen'inmaru Garden (Kanazawa) – restored strolling garden within Kanazawa Castle grounds; designed for seasonal viewing.

Myoryu-ji (Ninja Temple) (Kanazawa) – hidden stairways and defensive tricks; built more for intrigue than ninja.

Oyama Shrine (Kanazawa) – an unusual Dutch-influenced gate; stained glass; East–West design fusion.

Shirayama Hime Jinja (Hakusan City) – shrine dedicated to Mount Hakusan, one of Japan's three sacred mountains; long linked to Yamabushi ascetic pilgrimages.

Teramachi Temple District (Kanazawa) – dozens of temples with hidden gardens; rakugo storytelling nights or kaidan (ghost-tale) performances; temple cuisine (shojin ryori).

HISTORIC PRECINCTS

Nagamachi Samurai District (Kanazawa) – preserved samurai precinct; narrow lanes; earthen walls; Nomura-ke samurai residence.

Higashi Chaya (Kanazawa) – best-preserved geisha entertainment quarter; teahouses; gold-leaf workshops; elegant cafes.

Nishi Chaya (Kanazawa) – smaller, less crowded; several active teahouses remain.

Kazuemachi Chaya (Kanazawa) – atmospheric lanes along the Asano River; wooden facades; lantern-lit evenings.

Kaga Onsen – historic hot spring towns; ceramics; lacquer; small artists' studios within walking distance of the baths.

Nanao – Castle ruins; oldtown street of Ipponsugi-dori's merchant stores.

Summer and winter scenes in Kenroku-en Garden, Kanazawa.

MUSEUMS, GALLERIES & CULTURAL LIFE

21st Century Museum of Contemporary Art (**Kanazawa**) – circular design; interactive exhibitions; international artists.

Kanazawa Noh Museum – preserving the city's Noh theatre heritage.

Ishikawa Prefectural Museum of Art (**Kanazawa**) – traditional arts; lacquerware; Kutani porcelain.

Ishikawa Prefectural Museum of Traditional Arts and Crafts (**Kanazawa**) – exhibiting 36 of the prefecture's master crafts; gold leaf; Wajima-nuri lacquerware; Nanao candles; shishimai masks.

Grassroots culture – a living creative undercurrent; indie galleries; student-led performances; seasonal pop-up shows; repurposed warehouses hosting collaborative exhibitions of ceramics, textiles and contemporary design.

TRADITIONAL CRAFTS & EXPERIENCES

Gold leaf workshops (**Kanazawa**) – nearly all of Japan's gold leaf is from this district; hands-on experiences; artisans; minimalist jewellery.

Wajima-nuri lacquerware studios (**Wajima**) – jet-black or deep vermillion in colour, both classic and contemporary.

Above: 21st Century Museum of Contemporary Art, Kanazawa.
Below: Suzu salt sheds at the sea's edge, Noto.

Kutani-yaki pottery (Kaga) – reimagined by younger ceramicists; traditional motifs in bold, modern forms.

Kaga-yuzen silk dyeing (Kaga) – kimono dyeing studios; demonstrations; short workshops.

Shishimai mask carving (Noto) – hand-carved lion-dance masks for festivals; occasional workshops.

Yunokuni no Mori (Komatsu) – forest crafts village under a canopy of workshops and studios; Wajima lacquerware; Kutani porcelain; gold leaf; washi paper; yuzen dyeing; glassblowing; tea ceremony; wagashi.

Takazawa Candle Shop (Nanao) – occasional open workshops; over 150 years of handpainted plant-wax candles.

Ishikawa Local Products Centre (Kanazawa) – craft and food shopping; experiences.

FESTIVALS & PERFORMANCE

Summer
Hyakumangoku Festival (Kanazawa, June) – commemorating Lord Maeda's entry to the castle; parades; performances.

Kiriko Festivals (Noto Peninsula, June to August) – towering lantern floats carried through the night; fire and drums echo through fishing villages.

Abare Festival, Noto (July) – 'Festival of Fire and Violence'; mikoshi (portable shrines) are smashed and set ablaze as fierce offerings to the gods.

Autumn
Kiriko Festivals (Noto Peninsula, September and October) – the rhythm of drums and fire continues.

Kenrokuen autumn illuminations (Kanazawa, November) – maple, Chrysanthemum, music and tea.

Winter
Shishimai lion dances – performed across Ishikawa to ward off evil and invite fortune; often led by local youth groups.

Gojinjo Daiko (Wajima) – drumming tradition performed only by locals; fierce masks and earth-shaking rhythms recalling wartime defiance; a cultural treasure.

Spring

Hanami (various locations, late March to early April) cherry-blossom-viewing festival and illuminations around Kanazaw'sa castle and Kenrokuen, Komatsu's Komaruyama Park, Daishoji Park.

Seihakusai Festival (Nanao, May) – giant dekayama floats pulled through the streets for protection and prosperity.

Kenrokuen Iris and Azalea season (Kanazawa, late May).

FOOD & DRINK

Kaga-ryori (cuisine) – refined multi-course traditions developed under Maeda clan patronage; a showcase of delicate seasonal seafood, heirloom vegetables, wild mountain greens. Specialities include Jibu-ni – rich local hotpot of duck, wheat gluten and vegetables, Gori no karaage (fried freshwater fish), Hasu-mushi – steamed lotus root and prawn paste, Kabura-zushi – pickled yellowtail pressed with turnip.

Seafood – snow crab; nodoguro (blackthroat seaperch); sweet shrimp; buri (yellowtail) in winter.

Omicho Market (Kanazawa) – local seafood, produce, and street foods; homely teishoku counters run by long-time vendors.

Above: Omicho seafood market snackery, Kanazawa.
Below: Nanao's Torii Shoyu-ten brewery, Noto.

Katamachi and Korinbo – Kanazawa's vibrant izakaya and dining precincts.

Kanazawa curry – cult local dish of thick, dark curry sauce, pork cutlet and shredded cabbage.

Hakui roadside stalls – produce and playful cosmic-themed souvenirs; coastal road settings.

Shojin ryori – Buddhist vegan cuisine; regional focus on sea vegetation and fermentation.

Noto's Satoumi culture – sustainable use of marine and coastal eco-systems – e.g. seaweed, Ishiri/Ishiru (locally fermented fish sauce used extensively).

Nanao's food shops – Ipponsugi street in atmospheric old quarter; seaweed specialists; long-standing miso and shoyu shops (some venues under repair or in temporary locations).

Family kitchens in Wajima – some open to visitors; hands-on experiences of making miso or pickles with grandmothers.

Suzu salt – Agehama-style salt-making; visitors sometimes join in the raking process.

Sake – community-owned breweries (some in repair) in Noto, known for its guild of master brewers. Hakusan's water supports Kaga sake's elegant style.

Wagashi – elegant sweets often garnished with gold leaf; tied to Kanazawa's tea culture.

NATURAL HIGHLIGHTS

Noto Peninsula – rugged coastlines; terraced rice paddies (Shiroyone Senmaida); salt fields.

Noto-jima – small, serene, wildlife-rich island connected by bridge to Nanao.

Mount Hakusan – sacred peak with alpine trails; Yamabushi lore; mountain faith.

Kakusenkei Gorge – runs through lush forest in Kaga; autumn foliage hikes.

Chirihama Nagisa Driveway – eight kilometres of drivable sandy beach; coastal rock formations tied to sea-god myths; surreal sunset drives.

Fukui (No. 18 – Total cities: 9)

Where dinosaur bones surface and monks sit in silence, Fukui holds distant eras within reach through patience and precision. At Eiheiji, days begin before dawn and are measured in sutras. In Echizen, washi is wind-dried, lacquer gleams from years of touch and knives are hand-hammered for balance. Winter hauls Echizen's famed snow crab from the Sea of Japan, and locals slurp oroshi soba and mountain greens. Tojinbo's cliffs plunge into rough surf. Mikata Five Lakes mirror seasonal beauty. Obama's temple roofs and narrow lanes hold the calm of a port once called 'Nara by the Sea'.

Yamanashi (No. 19 – Total cities: 13)

Landlocked yet abundant, 'Fruit Kingdom' Yamanashi rests at Fuji's feet. The mountain rises

Above: Take a fun pitstop in Nagano's Kamakura (igloo).
Below: Soak in the charm of Gifu's Takayama.

over Fujiyoshida and the Fuji Five Lakes, where ryokan and hot spring baths soothe hikers after the Yoshida Trail or autumn walks through the Southern Alps and Shosenkyo Gorge, fuelled by hearty Hoto stew. In Kofu, Takeda Shrine recalls the samurai age, and workshops still lacquer deerskin into patterned Inden. In Katsunuma, rows of Koshu vines climb the slopes of Japan's oldest wine country, while nearby artisans dye cloth in the itajime style and fire rustic pottery.

Nagano (No. 20 – Total cities: 19)

Nagano's beauty lies not only in its alpine slopes, alive with ski runs and onsen resorts, but in the Kiso Valley's Nakasendo trail towns of Narai-juku and Tsumago-juku, and in Shinshu's craft and cuisine. Roadside markets feature apples, grapes and wasabi alongside oyaki dumplings, hand-cut soba and chestnut sweets. Matsumoto's black castle anchors a city of galleries and quiet streets. Zenko-ji's bells call pilgrims into Nagano City. In Obuse, Hokusai's brushwork legacy lingers.

Gifu (No. 21 – Total cities: 21)

Gifu shows its mountain heart in torchlit rivers where cormorants dive, in the steep farmhouses of UNESCO World Heritage site Shirakawa-go, and in soulful wares including Mino's hand-crafted washi and pottery and Takayama's black-and-vermilion Hida Shunkei lacquerware. Takayama hums with morning markets, sake breweries and festival floats trundling along historic Sanmachi Suji's lanes. Ropeways climb into the frosty Alps, while the valleys are warm with onsen. Grilled Hida Beef and Gohei mochi's sweet-savoury smoke permeate the mountain air. Breathe deep.

Shizuoka (No. 22 – Total cities: 23)

Shizuoka sits alongside the Pacific, under the gaze of Fuji-san, who is more spirit than landmark, guarding abundant tea fields, wasabi streams and mandarin groves. From the same restless waves surfed by locals in Suruga Bay, shrimp and whitebait are hauled. The Izu Peninsula unwinds in hot-spring resorts and blossom-scattered coastal trails while the rhythm of travellers, past and present, mark the Old Tokaido road in the towns of Kanbara and Mariko, where streets are still lined with bamboo weaving, woodblock prints and pots of simmering oden.

Aichi (No. 23 – Total cities: 38)

Aichi is an industrial powerhouse and cultural crossroads where sacred shrines, artisan quarters and historic castle towns with blissful gardens, such as Nagoya and Inuyama, sit alongside the birthplace of Japan's automotive and aerospace industries. Aichi's vibrant Triennale art festival celebrates contemporary art, while Tokoname and Seto pottery villages honour their craft heritage. The region is sustained by robust miso-cuisine and complementary sake, and folklore – from white fox spirits to the Honen fertility festival, and riverside purification rituals.

Preserved Arimatsu Shibori Kaido (an indigo-lined stretch of the old Tokaido Road).

REGION 5.

Kansai/Kinki
(7 prefectures:
Mie, Shiga, Kyoto,
Osaka, Hyogo,
Nara, Wakayama)

Mie (No. 24 – Total cities: 14)

Mie wears spirituality like its finely woven Momen cotton garments – strong, practical and lived-in. Sun goddess Amaterasu is worshipped at Ise Jingu, and pilgrims tread Kumano Kodo's cedar-lined paths. Octogenarian Ama pearl divers descend into myth while ninja lore endures in Iga around the Akame 48 Waterfalls. Devotion threads through daily life: ryokan kneel along the coast, onsen bless slopes and valleys, Matsusaka's beef is immaculately charred and sweet Ise-Shima seafood provokes quiet gratitude.

Shiga (No. 25 – Total cities: 13)

Encircling Lake Biwa, Japan's largest freshwater lake, Shiga is shaped by water, trade and devotion. From canal towns and Omi merchant legacies to lake-born foods, lifestyle remains closely tied to Biwa-ko. More understated than its famous neighbour Kyoto, Shiga is culturally rich yet humble, a place where the avant-garde MIHO Museum coexists with Shigaraki's ancient pottery kilns, Nagahama's plum-bonsai festival, and rituals at Mount Hiei's Enryaku-ji. Tales of dragon gods, Koga ninja mischief and water spirits whisper through reed beds and shrine groves.

Above: Toba's oyster and pearl farms, Mie.
Below: Otsu's Sanno Matsuri parades towards Lake Biwa's edge, Shiga.

Kyoto
(No. 26 – Total cities: 15)

Kyoto prefecture is a meditation on continuity, holding past and present together with quiet grace. Its capital vibrates with the essence of more than a thousand years of emperors, monks and artisans, held in its stonework, laneways, gardens and festivals. Inland, temple bells, tofu carts and lantern-lined alleys speak to its imperial heart. Northward, satoyama fields give way to thatched hamlets and a rugged coast of fishing villages and pine-fringed bays. Kyoto breathes with the seasons – blossoms, bonfires, moonlit shrines and bamboo groves – while markets, freshly whisked matcha and quiet jazz bars are reminders that history and the present are constant companions.

Evening scenes in the geisha quarters of Gion and Pontocho.

CITIES, TOWNS & VILLAGES

Kyoto City (capital) – imperial legacy; vast temple and shrine complexes; geiko/maiko (geisha) districts; a multitude of arts, crafts, gardens and historic streets and lanes including the famous Ninenzaka and Sannenzaka slopes; deep tea and cafe culture; plentiful ryokan and machiya accommodation; Kyoto Station's futuristic architecture; university quarters around Ichijoji/Demachiyanagi – bohemian cafes, ramen haunts and student culture; Kiyamachi and Pontocho – riverside nightlife, izakaya, bars, jazz and performance spaces; Kamogawa – riverside walks and seasonal picnics, music; Kitayama – French-influenced enclave leaning into farmland at the foot of the northern mountains; Nishijin's textile workshops and craft studios; Okazaki's museum and gallery precinct.

Uji – Byodoin Temple; Ujigami Shrine; birthplace of matcha culture; wagashi traditions; Mimuroto-ji hydrangeas.

Fushimi – Fushimi-Inari Shrine's red torii trails; historic sake breweries; cherry-lined canals; seasonal boat rides.

Kameoka – Sagano Romantic Train; Hozu River boat rides; countryside scenery.

Nagaoka-kyo – temporary capital (784–794); Nagaoka Tenmangu Shrine (famous for azaleas and seasonal festivals); Komyo-ji Temple (autumn maples); quiet bamboo paths including the Nagaoka Bamboo Grove (and adjacent Muko city's Take-no-Michi bamboo trail).

Miyama – thatched kayabuki houses; snow igloos (kamakura); indigo craft; folk museum; shrines; ecotourism programs with rice planting and harvesting activities.

Ohara – Satoyama farming; Sanzen-in, Jakko-in and Hosen-in temples; farmers' markets; crafts; ryokan stays.

Northern Kyoto Mountains – Keihoku and Hanase – indigo workshops; farming; Yamabushi (ascetic practices); forestry culture; lush riverside; hiking and winter snowscapes.

Kurama and Kibune – mystical temple and shrine villages; water oracles; mountain trails; Tengu spirits; summertime somen at riverside dining platforms (kawadoko); onsen.

Kyotango – Kyoto by the sea; Amanohashidate sandbar; Ine funaya boathouses; Tango chirimen textiles.

TEMPLES, SHRINES & GARDENS

Central
Kennin-ji; Yasaka-jinja; Heian-jingu; Shoren-in; Murin-an; Rokkaku-do (ikebana origins); Kyoto Gyoen National Garden; Nijo-jo; Shinsen-en; Nishi and Higashi Honganji; Bukko-ji.

North/north-east
Ginkaku-ji; Daitoku-ji; Sanzen-in; Jakko-in; Hosen-in; Manshu-in; Shisen-do; Kamigamo-jinja; Kyoto Botanical Garden; Shoden-ji; Genko-an; Shugaku-in; Kibune-jinja; Kurama-dera; Tanuki-dani Fudo-in; Enko-ji; Hiei-san Enryuku-ji; Raigo-ji; Bujo-ji.

South/south-east/south-west
To-ji; Fushimi inari taisha; Tofuku-ji; Daigo-ji; Komyo-ji.

East
Nanzen-ji; Kiyomizu-dera; Kodai-ji; Konkai Komyo-ji (Shigemori Mirei gardens); Eikan-do; Chion-in; Maruyama Park; Byodoin; Oharano-jinja.

West
Kinkaku-ji; Tenry-ji; Okochi Sanso (movie-star villa, gardens and teahouse); Jojakko-ji; Arashiyama Bamboo forest; Ryoan-ji; Tenryu-ji; Myoshin-ji; Taizo-in; Otagi Nenbutsu-ji; Adashino Nenbutsu-ji; Matsuo-taisha; Saiho-ji (Kokedera); Daikaku-ji; Nison-in; Atago-jinja.

Seasonal flowers and illuminations
Sakura at Maruyama Park; the Philosopher's Path, along the Kamogawa and various canals; plum blossoms at Kitano Tenmangu; irises at Heian-jingu; hydrangeas at Sanzen-in and Mimuroto-ji; lotuses at To-ji and Shinnyo-do; fiery maples at Tofuku-ji and Eikando; camellias in winter gardens; various seasonal temple illuminations.

Above: The serene grounds of Sanzen-in, Ohara.
Below: Observant, shape-shifting Tanuki.

HISTORIC PRECINCTS

Kyoto city

Kyoto Gosho – Imperial Palace and tranquil park and garden precinct.

Nijo-jo Castle – impressive halls, screens, scrolls and gardens, 'nightingale' floors; Nijo-jinya old samurai residence; Ninja history.

Daitoku-ji and Myoshin-ji – sprawling temple towns and intimate gardens.

Hanamachi (flower-towns or geiko quarters) of Gion Kobu, Gion Higashi, Pontocho, Kamishichiken, Miyagawacho.

Ninenzaka & Sannenzaka – legendary slopes around Kiyomizu-dera, lined with former merchant houses, now shops, restaurants, galleries, museums.

Shirakawa Canal district (Shirakawa-minami dori) – willow-lined canal, bridges and teahouses; nearby Shinmonzen dori for antiques.

Nishijin – traditional weaving/textile merchant precinct; old shophouses.

Teramachi – former temple strip; northern end (above Oike dori) antiques and traditional crafts, e.g. washi, tin, tea, etc.

Further afield

Kameoka (west) – Shoryuji castle ruins; old merchant houses.

Miyama (north-west) – preserved thatched roof farmhouse village and community.

Kyo-Tango and Ine (north-west) – Miyazu's castle town and ports; Ine's photogenic preserved boat houses; national heritage district.

Nagaokakyo (south-west) – castle ruins and serene merchant streets.

Oharano (south-west) – mossy temple and shrine valleys, rustic inns.

Fushimi (south-east) – canals and old sake brewing district.

Uji (south-east) – temple town; Omotesando street, tea lanes.

Tanba-Sasayama (north-west) – excellent daytrip over the Hyogo border (Tanba formerly in Kyoto); castle town; samurai precinct; Tanba pottery; Edo-period streetscapes.

Above: Ninenzaka slope in Higashiyama.
Below: Relaxing by the Kamogawa (river).

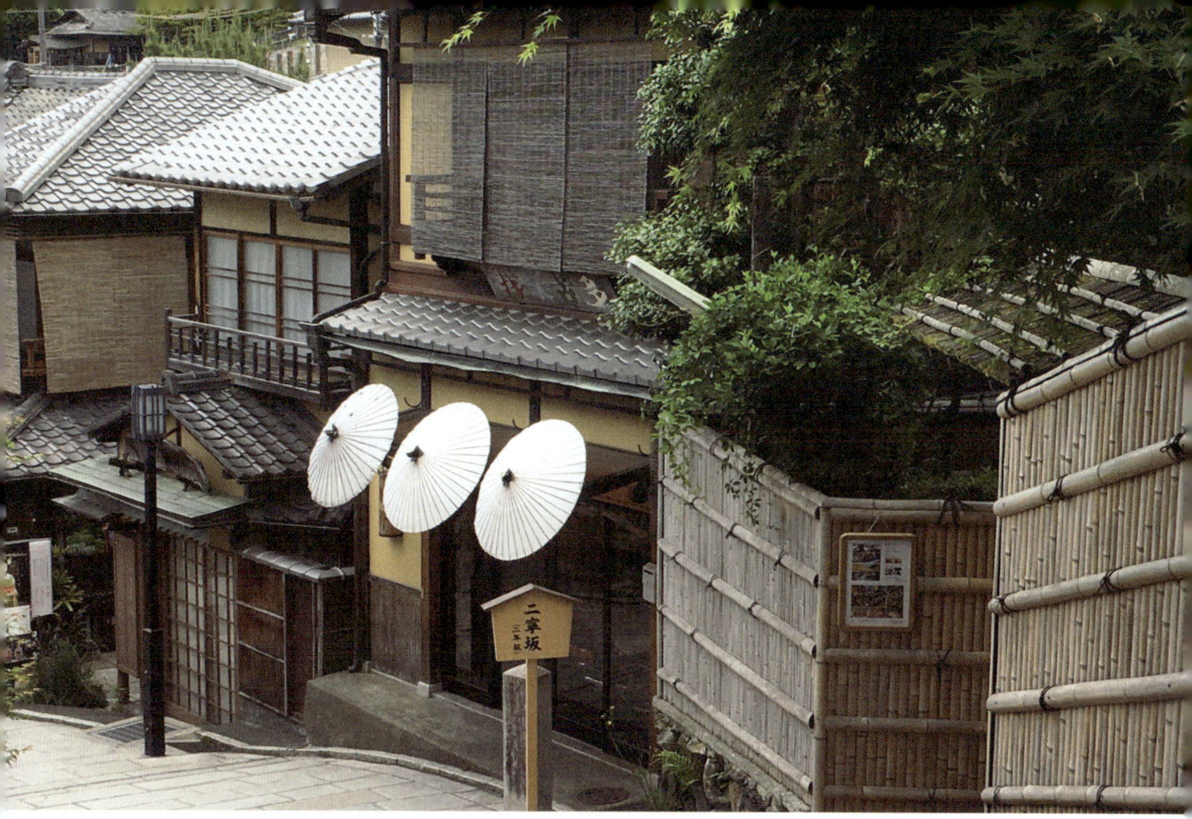
二寧坂
(三年坂)

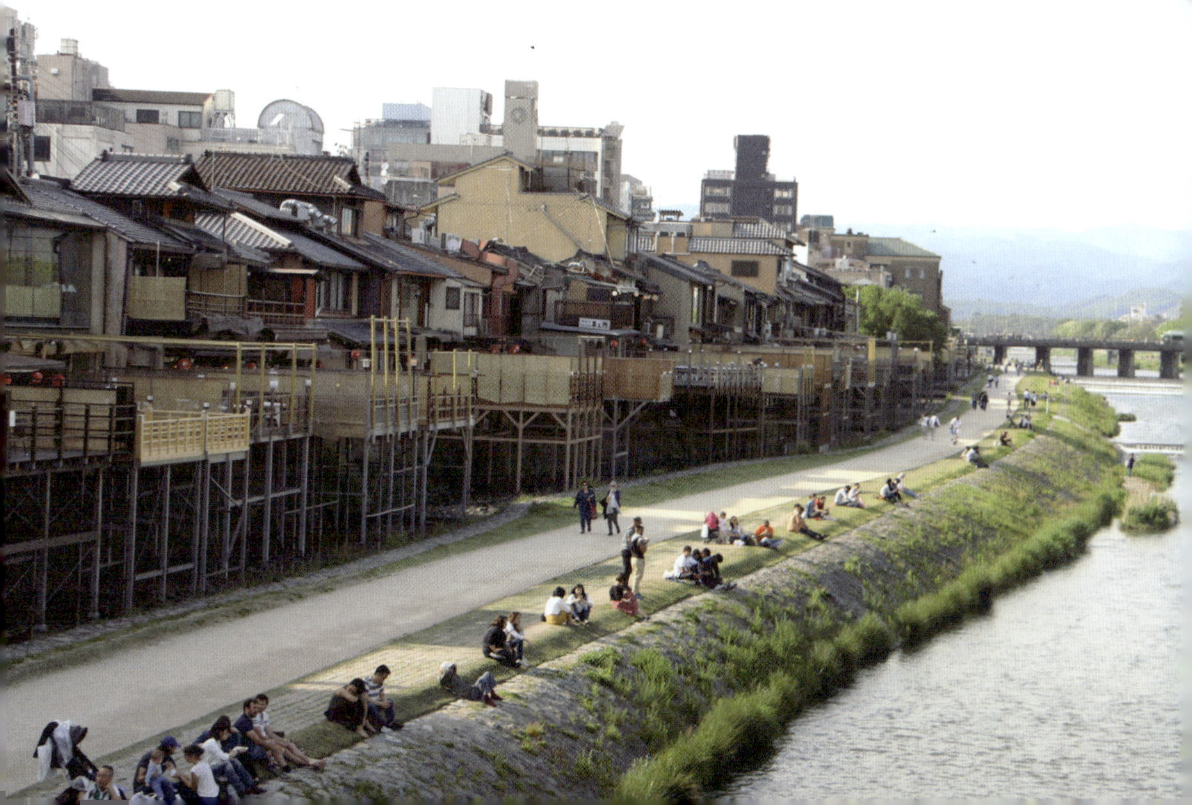

MUSEUMS, GALLERIES & CULTURAL LIFE

Okazaki museum district – Hosomi Museum; KYOCERA Museum of Art; MOMAK (National Museum of Modern Art); Kyoto Museum of Craft and Design. Elsewhere: Kyoto National Museum; Kyoto International Manga Museum; Raku Museum; Kahitsukan contemporary art museum; Kawai Kanjiro House; Kyoto Art Center's multidisciplinary hub; KYOTOGRAPHIE photography festival; small ateliers in restored townhouses, some connected to students and alumni of Kyoto City University of Arts and Kyoto Seika University.

Sento culture – traditional neighbourhood public baths (older homes without baths still use these, most are not onsen (natural hotsprings) but some onsen exist in Kurama, Arashiyama and Kameoka).

Supernatural – everyday conversations around ghosts and spirit; ley lines; eerie tales and a meeting of worlds linked to Midorigaike Pond, the Kamogawa's banks, Senbon dori, Ichijo dori and beyond; Taishogun Yokai street – grassroots cultural project inspired by Kyoto's yokai (spirits, ghosts, etc.) legends.

Regular markets – a blend of pilgrimage and community gathering; flea and antiques; To-ji's Kobo-san (on the 21st of each month); Kitano Tenmangu's Tenjin-san (on the 25th of each month); Garakuta-ichi (flea) (first Sunday of the

month); Chion-ji's tezukuri (handmade craft) market (15th of the month); Kamigamo-jinja (4th Sunday of the month); Shimogama (seasonal tezukuri); Okazaki Park (irregular dates).

TRADITIONAL CRAFTS & EXPERIENCES

Crafts – Kiyomizu pottery; Nishijin textiles; Kyo-yuzen kimono dyeing; Kyo-sensu folding fans; mokuhanga woodblock prints; karagami paper prints; netsuke carvings; Kyo-shikki lacquerware; washi paper; indigo dyeing in Kyoto city, Miyama and Keihoku; incense workshops at Shoyeido and Lisn; ikebana; kintsugi (gold repair); Kyo-kinko metalcraft experiences available.

Kyoto Handicraft Center (Okazaki, near Heian-jingu) – multi-floor centre; demonstrations and shops; Kyoto's crafts.

Kyoto Museum of Crafts and Design (Miyako Messe, Okazaki) – showcases all 74 officially recognised traditional crafts of Kyoto; live demonstrations; curated exhibits.

Kyomachiya galleries and studios – reimagined townhouses as intimate spaces for artists, designers and potters to display work.

Antiques – clusters around northern Teramachi; Shinmonzen dori and Nawate dori antiques streets; Ebisu-gawa dori for antique (and modern) furniture.

Above: Shinsen-do.
Below: Kiyomizu-dera.

FESTIVALS & PERFORMANCE

Summer

Gion Matsuri (**July**) – enormous festival and processions.

Gozan Okuribi (**August**) – bonfires on Daimonji and nearby mountains to farewell ancestral spirits who visit during Obon (essentially, a festival of the dead).

Kawadoko (**Yuka**) (**May–September**) – temporary deck dining over Kamogawa and Kibune rivers.

Takatsuki Jazz Street festival (**May**) – free popular live jazz stages.

Autumn

Jidai Matsuri (**October**) – period costume procession marking Kyoto's founding.

Kurama Fire Festival (**October**) – torches light up mountain streets.

Tsukimi (**September–October**) – moon-viewing rituals with dango and sake, various locations.

Autumn Leaf illuminations (**November**) – various.

Winter

Illuminations – including Arashiyama Hanatouro lantern festival; Kamakura light-ups in Miyama.

O-shogatsu (**end December–early January**) – New Year's festival; joya no okane temple bell ringing in evening of 31st;

Above: Arashiyama's bamboo forest.
Below: Period costume, Aoi Matsuri.

Hatsumode – first shrine visit (1–3 January).

Setsubun (February) – bean-throwing rituals to banish demons (Kamigamo-jinja); bonfires at Yoshida-jinja; Yasaka Jin-ja; Oni (demon) festivals on Tango Peninsula.

Baikai-sai (February) – plum blossom festival in Kitano Tenmangu grounds.

Spring

Aoi Matsuri (May) – Heian period court procession.

Hanami (late March/early April) – blossom-viewing picnics along the Kamogawa, Maruyama park; evening illuminations – various.

Miyako odori (April) – spring geiko dance performed at Gion Kobu.

Performance culture – Minami-za Theatre for kabuki; Nihon-buyo traditional dance (Kaburenjo theatres around Geisha quarters and at festivals); Butoh experimental dance theatre (Butoh-kan is one dedicated venue); experimental live arts at UrBANGUILD; eclectic mix of traditional and futuristic performance at ROHM theatre, e.g. Kyoto experiment (performing arts festival).

Jazz and live houses – intimate venues and student-driven clubs in Kiyamachi and Demachiyanagi, reflecting Kyoto's quiet status as a jazz capital.

FOOD & DRINK

Kyo-ryori – seasonal cuisine including obanzai dishes; Kyo-yasai (revered local vegetables); guji fish (tilefish); chirimen jakko (tiny sardines with sansho); sabazushi (vinegared mackerel sushi); tsukemono (pickles); tofu in various forms; shojin ryori (Buddhist vegan cuisine); kaiseki dining at ryotei/ryokan.

Food markets – Nishiki Market; Kyoto Central Wholesale Market; Demachi-masuga shotengai (Demachiyanagi); Sanjo Shotengai (Sanjo dori near Nijo station); Ohara's Asa-ichi farmers' market; and several great depachika (subterranean department-store food halls), e.g. Daimaru, Takashimaya.

Tea culture (chado/sado) – matcha from Uji; Camellia Tea Ceremony; tea and wagashi houses/salons, e.g. – Ippodo, Toraya salon (seasonal sweets – sakura mochi, hydrangea nerikiri, moon-viewing dango, chestnut confections); sleek, contemporary tea omakase.

Izakaya precincts – Ponto-cho; Kiyamachi-dori; Gion backstreets; Nishiki-koji backstreets; Fushimi; station areas around Demachiyanagi/Ichijoji, Shijo-Karasuma Kawaramachi-Sanjo, Omiya and Saiin.

Ramen alleys – Kyoto Station's Ramen Koji; student haunts near the universities; Ichijoji Ramen Street, known locally as the city's ramen heartland.

Gin and sake – Kyoto Distillery (Ki No Bi), the home of Japan's first craft gin using Fushimi water and local botanicals; Kyoto Miyako Distillery's Kyoto Gin with matcha and Japanese cinnamon; the Fushimi district's historic sake breweries.

Cafe culture – nostalgic kissaten and sleek modern roasters; historic Inoda Coffee and Ogawa Coffee representing Kyoto's long-standing cafe traditions; many tiny local roasters reflecting the city's contemporary edge.

Yoshoku cafes – not unique to Kyoto, but part of the city's dining rhythm; Teramachi's Smart Coffee is a retro institution, serving fluffy hotcakes, omurice and Napolitan spaghetti beneath chandeliers and wood-panelled walls since 1932.

Obanzai alleys – homely Kyoto-style comfort food counter eateries in lanes found around Kiyamachi, Pontocho, Omiya and Nijo-jo.

NATURAL HIGHLIGHTS

Arashiyama/Kameoka – Hozu River boat rides; Sagano Romantic Railway for seasonal foliage viewings.

Mount Daimonji – gentle hiking with panoramic city views.

Higashiyama walking trails – linking Ginkaku-ji to Nanzen-ji via Philosopher's walk (tetsugaku no michi).

Kurama–Kibune – mountain pilgrimage route; hot springs; cedar forest.

Mount Hiei (Hieizan) temple – mountain hikes to Enryakuji complex; Biwa views; cablecar.

Takao and Atago-yama – fire-prevention pilgrim routes with brilliant autumn foliage.

Northern Kyoto mountains – Miyama, Keihoku & Hanase, with winter snowscapes; Hanase riverside walks and fishing.

Ohara – picturesque farming lands and temple trails.

Tango Peninsula – rugged Sea of Japan coast, sea caves, sandy coves, misty inlets, scenic drives.

Oharano – ancient forest, shrine woods, sacred paths.

Above: Yudofu in nabe pot.
Below: Quaint Miyama village.

Osaka (No. 27 – Total cities: 33)

A prefecture known for its youth-culture, appetite, comedy and restless invention, Osaka sizzles in the kitchen and on stage. Neon streets buzz with takoyaki banter and glitzy retail. Beyond the modern city are Sakai's samurai tombs and blade-forging fame, Minoh's waterfalls, the tea fields of Nose, and Osaka Bay's fishing villages and family-friendly theme parks. From merchant knives to bunraku puppets, rakugo punchlines to baseball chants, Osaka thrives on trade, humour and performance.

Hyogo (No. 28 – Total cities: 29)

Cosmopolitan and worldly but grounded, Hyogo swaggers from point to point: Kobe's live houses, Takarazuka's glittering entertainment, Tamba-Sasayama's Edo streetscapes and pottery, Himeji's white castle, Izushi's ghost-haunted lanes and Kinosaki's onsen-focused ryokan. Its story is of crossings and connections – trade routes through the Seto, bridges to Shikoku, and international ports. In the highlands, wagyu graze, while storks ponder Toyooka's wetlands and, along the coastline of Awaji Island, myth and incense drift across flower fields.

Nara (No. 29 – Total cities: 12)

Where the first flowering of Buddhism met Silk Road currents, forests and peaks were enshrined as gods. Myth and history entwine in the burial mounds and megaliths of Futago Kofun and Asuka, Horyu-ji's sacred halls, Yoshino's sakura-clad slopes,

Nara city's Great Buddha precinct and preserved Naramachi old town lanes. Plum grove perfumed valleys reverberate with horns and conch shells where deer gather and Yamabushi walk. Fire rituals blaze in temple courts and local sake and somen are offered to the gods of Mount Miwa.

Wakayama (No. 30 – Total cities: 9)

At the southern edge of the Kii Peninsula, Wakayama climbs steeply from a wild Pacific shore. Pilgrimage routes weave through temple towns and fishing ports, monks chant at mystical Koyasan, and water carries rites of purification and passage at thundering Nachi Falls. Along the coast, tuna auctions break dawn's silence, plums ripen on Kishu's terraced hillsides destined for umeshu, and temple-inn onsen restore body, mind and spirit.

Above: Dotombori, Osaka City.
Below: Morning deer! Sustaining Nara Park's sacred critters.

REGION 6.

Chugoku
(5 prefectures: Tottori, Shimane, Okayama, Hiroshima, Yamaguchi)

Tottori (No. 31 – Total cities: 4)

The smallest prefecture in the region by population, but weighty with folklore and myth, Tottori is sculpted by sand and story. Inland Mount Daisen's spiritual axis invites sacred sojourns. Townships whisper tales of the White Hare of Inaba and Shigeru Mizuki's yokai. People commune where Kurayoshi's pear orchards turn the plains white each spring. The Karoichi Fish Market, healing onsen villages and windswept sand dunes are also important gathering places. Expansive yet intimate, Tottori offers elemental landscapes and encounters that linger.

Shimane (No. 32 – Total cities: 8)

Often called the spiritual birthplace of Japan, Shimane rests on Honshu's west coast with quiet gravitas – less spectacle than presence. Washi, lacquer, iron and clay still shape daily life, while Izumo myths and Oki Islands' lore inspire ritual and gathering. Shimane's spirit is felt everywhere, from Izumo Taisha's great shrine and fire festivals to Adachi's sublime gardens, Iwami Ginzan's silver pathways, Matsue's serene tearooms and Lake Shinji's breathtaking sunsets, which are best viewed from an open-air bath (rotenburo).

Adachi Museum of Art and Gardens, Shimane. *Image credit: Yuko Nakao.*

Okayama
(No. 33 – Total cities: 15)

Lying between the Chugoku Mountains and the Seto Inland Sea, Okayama is a prefecture of white peach orchards, grape vines, kilns and canals where legend and craft connect. Kurashiki's willow-lined waterways, Bizen's fire-marked pottery and the dairy-rich Hiruzen Highlands speak of place and tradition. In the capital, Okayama Castle and Korakuen Garden anchor a city of markets, shotengai and museums. With ferries linking directly to Naoshima, Teshima and Inujima, the prefecture also nods knowingly towards the arts.

Above: Edo period streetscape, Kurashiki.
Below: Okayama castle perched above Koraku-en.

CITIES, TOWNS & VILLAGES

Okayama (capital) – riverside castle town with its identity shaped by Okayama Castle and Koraku-en (garden); heartland of the Momotaro (peach boy) legend that you'll see echoed in local shrines, annual festivals and the sweet rice dumplings (kibi dango) sold across town; Omotecho Shopping Street hums with daily life; Thursday growers' markets and the Kyobashi Morning Market keep food traditions lively; indie cafes; galleries; Uno Port's ferries to the Setouchi art islands link the city to wider currents of creativity.

Kurashiki – canal-side willow trees and white-walled kura framing the Bikan Quarter, once tied to the rice trade and now alive with antique stalls, machiya lodgings and book cafes; a balance between Edo nostalgia and creative energy; a city synonymous with denim and indigo workshops.

Tsuyama – castle town framed by mountains; best known for cherry blossoms that sweep across ruins and parks in spring; farmers' markets brimming with mountain produce; community kitchens that keep food traditions close.

Mimasaka and Yubara – slower-paced rural mountain valleys with hot spring ryokan, riverside baths, and farmstays; samurai lore; seasonal cooking; forested landscapes.

Bizen – industrious kilns and clay workshops of Bizen's villages preserving one of Japan's oldest ceramic lineages; earthy and tactile atmosphere; potters' markets add to the sense of living tradition.

Maniwa and Hiruzen Highlands – highland meadows dotted with dairy farms, flower parks and cycling trails; summer breezes scented with lilies; quiet winter snow slopes; Jersey-milk sweets; rustic warmth.

Takahashi (Bitchu Matsuyama) Castle – castle town; mist rises from the valleys at dawn; samurai streets; local markets; mountaintop fortress; an almost timeless landscape.

Ushimado – coastal town sometimes called 'Japan's Aegean'; known for fishing hamlets, olive groves and hillside views across the Seto Inland Sea; fishermen's boats take visitors onto the water.

Tamano – home to the Setouchi's vital Uno Port; chilled seaside cafes; hints of Setouchi art.

TEMPLES, SHRINES & GARDENS

Koraku-en – one of Japan's Three Great Gardens; a spacious daimyo retreat; ponds, streams and seasonal colour set against the backdrop of Okayama Castle across the Asahi River.

Kibitsujinja Shrine – linked to the Momotaro legend; long covered corridor; ritual traditions.

Bitchu Kokubun-ji – historic temple; striking five-storey pagoda; rice-field setting.

HISTORIC PRECINCTS

Okayama Castle – nicknamed 'Crow Castle' for its black-lacquered walls; golden Shachihoko roof ornaments; exhibits on daimyo culture and Bizen pottery; seasonal boat rides circling the moat.

Tsuyama Castle ruins – revered hanami site; sweeping cherry blossom views.

Kurashiki Bikan Quarter – Edo-period merchant streets and canals; waterways lined by kura and willows.

Bitchu Matsuyama Castle – an original mountaintop fortress; spectacular in autumn mornings, emerging from a sea of clouds.

Katsuyama Historical Preservation District – post town on the old Izumo kaido road; whitewalled kura (storehouses); artful noren signage.

Imbe – historic heart of Bizen-yaki pottery; Edo-era climbing kilns and clay storehouses; festivals; small museums.

MUSEUMS, GALLERIES & CULTURAL LIFE

Ohara Museum of Art (Kurashiki) – Japan's first private Western art museum; collection includes Monet, El Greco and Japanese masters.

Okayama Prefectural Museum of Art – refined showcase of regional works; light-filled modernist setting.

Kurashiki Folk-craft Museum – mingei movement crafts; handsome kura setting.

Bizen Osafune Sword Museum – swordsmithing exhibitions; live demonstrations.

Kurashiki Archaeological Museum – local history; excavated artefacts.

Yubara Onsen Museum – a living record of a mountain onsen community.

Okayama Orient Museum – Middle Eastern and Islamic art; a rare collection.

Mizushima Industrial Zone nightscape tours – guided night views of the industrial complex; surreal scenes beloved by photographers.

Kurashiki Ivy Square Cultural Hub – former spinning mill; exhibitions; design fairs; creative residencies.

Setouchi Triennale connection – ferries from Okayama link directly to Naoshima, Teshima and Inujima; a gateway to Japan's celebrated art islands.

Above: Imbe, Bizen.
Below: Kurashiki Bikan's canal ways.

TRADITIONAL CRAFTS & EXPERIENCES

Bizen-yaki pottery – unglazed, flame-marked ceramics; iron-rust hues; potters offer hands-on sessions and markets.

Kurashiki denim and indigo – globally renowned deep indigo dye and durable weave; ateliers run dyeing workshops and jeans-making experiences.

Swordsmithing (Osafune) – forging and polishing workshops and demonstrations; carrying on samurai-era traditions.

Tatara ironmaking heritage (Mimasaka) – small tool and craft workshops evoking the prefecture's mountain-forged steel traditions.

Kibi dango workshops (Okayama city) – sweet rice dumplings; Momotaro legend origins.

Kurashiki mingei – folk craft shops; textiles, ceramics and lacquerware; a celebration of the mingei movement.

Washi papermaking (northern villages) – small rural studios; keeping handmade paper alive.

FESTIVALS & PERFORMANCE

Summer
Kurashiki Tenryo Festival (July) – elegant lantern processions and dance celebrate Edo-period prosperity.

Okayama Momotaro Festival (August) – parades; dance troupes; fireworks.

Bitchu Takahashi Summer Fireworks Festival (September) – magnificent music-synced hanabi (fireworks) over the Takahashi River.

Kasaoka Bay's Sunflower fields – a golden sea of sunshine.

Autumn
Bizen Pottery Festival (Imbe, Bizen City) (October) – artisan-filled streets; glowing kilns.

Tsuyama matsutake mushroom events (September–November) – seasonal markets; tastings of fragrant, truffle-like matsutake.

Autumn foliage (late October–mid November) – magnificent views and harvest festivals (Hiruzen Highlands); Okutsu Momiji Matsuri festival and walks (Okutsu Gorge).

Kibiji Kagura (September–March) – Momotaro-related folk dance performed at lantern-lit shrines around Kibitsu.

Winter
Oyster festivals (January–March) (Seto Inland Sea coastline) – oysters in peak season; celebrated at Hinase, Ushimado, Kasaoka.

Hiruzen Yukoi Festival (Hiruzen Highlands) – snow festival: igloos, sledding, snowshoeing and illuminations.

Kibiji Kagura folk dance (September to March)

Hadaka Matsuri (Saidaiji Kannon-in, February) – naked festival; frenzied water purification ritual.

Spring
Tsuyama Cherry Blossom Festival (Kakuzan Park) (late March–early April) – 1000 cherry trees, udon stalls, music, tea, performance.

Peach blossom appreciation (Okayama City) (March) – sweetly perfumed blossoms; flower-viewing orchard strolls; photography.

FOOD & DRINK

White peaches and Pione grapes – Okayama's most celebrated produce, enjoyed fresh in summer and autumn; featured in parfait cafes across the

Art and craft mixed into the everyday in Kurashiki and Bizen.

prefecture; the centrepiece of seasonal festivals and sweets.

Matsutake mushrooms – prized autumn delicacy; from Tsuyama's mountains.

Oysters – harvested from the Seto Inland Sea; served in rustic huts.

Dairy – Hiruzen Highlands' best; Jersey milk; cheese; yoghurt; sweets.

Kibi dango – Momotaro's rice dumplings; handmade and sold as local souvenirs.

Okayama barazushi – colourful pressed sushi; seasonal toppings.

Okayama ramen – soy and chicken broth; hearty and local.

Tsuyama horumon udon – hearty noodles with pork offal in soy or miso broth.

Hiruzen yakisoba – stirfried noodles with local chicken and cabbage.

Hinase kakioko – local-style okonomiyaki with oysters.

Chiya Beef – tender wagyu from Niimi; served grilled (yakinku), over rice (gyudon), in sukiyaki or shabu-shabu.

Sansai okowa – rice with wild mountain greens.

Sake – strong culture showcased in breweries across Okayama, especially in Kurashiki and the Kanzakigawa district; Japan's oldest sake rice strain, Omachi rice; tastings in atmospheric sake kura (brewery) streets.

Above: Golden fields of Chayamachi.
Below: Imbe homes and pottery studios, Bizen.

Community cooking gatherings – with local obaachan (grannies); matsutake rice, barazushi and other seasonal dishes.

Michi-no-Eki, various, including Sainai Chaya (Mimasaka) – local produce and specialities, e.g. black bean ice cream, homemade fare; Kasaoka Bay Farm's white peach smoothie.

Olive groves – tastings above the Seto Inland Sea with Mediterranean-style views in Ushimado.

NATURAL HIGHLIGHTS

Hiruzen Highlands – skiing in winter; cycling; flower fields; farm festivals in summer.

Washuzen Highand/Shimotsui – coastal cliffs; panoramic Seto views.

Chugoku Mountains – trails; waterfalls; hidden shrines.

Kibji Plains – historic cycling route; kofun burial mounds.

Yubara Onsen – riverside baths; mountain views; nearby forest bathing.

Seto Inland Sea – ferries to Naoshima, Teshima and other art islands.

Takahashi River – scenic boating and cycling through peach orchards, misty valleys.

Seto Ohashi Bridge – 13-kilometre-long, double-decker engineering marvel linking Okayama to Shikoku's Takamatsu city, by rail or car, across the Setouchi (Seto Inland Sea).

Hiroshima (No. 34 – Total cities: 14)

Hiroshima stretches from the salt-sprayed Seto Inland Sea to the cedar-shadowed Chugoku Mountains, where gorges offer cool shade and remembrance meets renewal. The capital city – rebuilt around the Peace Memorial Park – pulses with rivers and trams. Not far away are Miyajima island's Itsukushima shrine and deer, the sake brewery streets of Saijo, and Setouchi ports like Onomichi and Tomonoura. The Shimanami Kaido (bridge/cycle route) links to Shikoku's Ehime across the Inland Sea. Local tables brim with oysters, noodle-packed okonomiyaki, bright citrus and sake.

Yamaguchi (No. 35 – Total cities: 13)

At Honshu's south-west tip, sea-swept coastlines with dramatic cliffs fringe a quietly confident Yamaguchi – more understated than its neighbours, yet robust in flavour. Hagi's elegant, preserved samurai quarter and tactile pottery, and the tranquil onsen village of Nagata Yumoto Onsen, contrast with seat-gripping coastal drives, Shimonoseki's pumping fish markets and famed fugu (pufferfish) cuisine. Mists drift across mountain plateaus, lending a mysterious air. Bridges and pedestrian tunnel crossings make Yamaguchi both a destination and a signpost between Honshu and Kyushu.

Above: Hiroshima's A-bomb dome peace memorial.
Below: Yamaguchi's coastline view across The Sea of Japan.

REGION 7.

Shikoku
(4 prefectures: Tokushima, Kagawa, Ehime, Kochi)

Tokushima (No. 36 – Total cities: 8)

At the island's north-eastern gateway, Tokushima (old Awa) swirls with Naruto (whirlpools), indigo vats and the exuberance of Awa Odori dance. Wasanbon sugar and sudachi citrus add subtler notes of place, while the Iya Valley's vine bridges, goblin tales and thatched hamlets preserve a mountain world that feels at once remote and deeply settled. Here, the Yoshino river surges through Oboke Gorge's slate cliffs, and folk songs draw the past into the present, much like modern-day pilgrims retrace history along the Henro 88 temple route.

Kagawa (No. 37 – Total cities: 8)

Japan's smallest prefecture sits at the heart of the Seto Inland Sea, with ferries and bridges linking Shikoku and the art islands to Honshu. Every three years the Setouchi Triennale transforms these waters. Beyond its role as a gateway, Kagawa's capital, Takamatsu, is a relaxed yet dynamic city of soulful shotengai and izakaya, and home to breathtakingly elegant Ritsurin gardens. Bonsai culture thrives in Kinashi and Kokubunji's centuries-old nurseries, while fishing hamlets align with contemporary installations. On Shodoshima layers of soy breweries, olive groves and sun-dried somen are intersected with art and yokai (monster) lanes. Traditions of Sanuki, the former name for Kagawa, still flavour the area's modern culture, and Udon.

Above: Wakimachi indigo town, Tokushima.
Below: Yayoi Kusama's pumpkin art, Naoshima.

Ehime
(No. 38 – Total cities: 11)

Ehime curves around Shikoku's south-western corner, looking out to both the Seto Inland and Uwa Seas. Terraced mikan orchards roll down towards the waterfront, while forested valleys look skywards to the Shikoku Karst, where cows graze and night skies shimmer. Matsuyama anchors the north with its castle and historic bathhouse culture. Riverside towns like Ozu and Uchiko beautifully revive preserved merchant streets. In the south, Uwajima blends fishing traditions, pearl farms and summer festivals. Ehime balances maritime energy with rural quiet, the slower pace allowing traditions to linger and creativity to reawaken.

Above: Ikazaki Kite Museum, Uchiko.
Below: Ehime's famous Mikan terraces.

CITIES, TOWNS & VILLAGES

Matsuyama City (**capital**) – castle town; trams running to Dogo Onsen, Japan's oldest hot spring; ghost stories and bathhouse legends; retro cafes and small galleries animate everyday life.

Imabari – gateway to the Shimanami Kaido (expressway and cycling route) linking Ehime with Hiroshima's charming Onomichi port town; views of Geiyo Islands' bridges; production of coveted Imabari towels.

Ozu and Uchiko – Ozu's riverside villas; handsome castle precinct; koi waterways; alluring merchant rows filled with craft and design shops, soy micro-breweries and cafes; Uchiko's Yokaichi–Gokoku district preserves wax and silk heritage; kabuki theatre.

Uwajima – a working port town where fishing, pearl culture, mikan farming and jokamachi (castle town) streets meet; summer festivals bring bull-sumo and ushi-oni (bull-demon) floats.

Saijo, Niihama and Shikokuchuo – inland-sea towns; autumn float and taiko festivals; family workshops still make washi and decorative mizuhiki paper cords bearing symbolic communication and wishes.

OUTLYING ISLANDS

Kashima – 3-minute ferry ride from northern Matsuyama's Hojo port; free roaming deer; white sand beaches; tranquil coastal trails.

Geiyo archipelago islands – Omishima, Hakatajima and Oshima islands relax in the shade of the Shimanami Kaido; pirate lore; shrines; salt production and workshops; citrus; beaches, cafes, cycling.

TEMPLES, SHRINES & GARDENS

Isaniwa Shrine (**Matsuyama**) – Hachiman-style shrine; ornate.

Ishite-ji (**Matsuyama**) – atmospheric Henro temple (no. 51); cave passages.

Tensha-en (**Uwajima**) – small but impactful daimyo stroll garden.

Garyu Sanso (**Ozu**) – villa and gardens; Hiji River setting; built for quiet retreat.

Taga Shrine (**Uwajima**) – fertility lore threaded through; amulets and rituals are sought with humour and reverence; adjacent sex museum.

HISTORIC PRECINCTS

Ozu Castle Town – restored castle and castle stays; riverside streets; new life in old merchant houses; Koi in waterways; shoyu breweries.

Uchiko Yokaichi–Gokoku District – preserved wax and silk heritage; antiques; local vinegar shop; Uchiko-za Kabuki Theatre; weekend markets.

Uwajima Castle Town – jokamachi; merchant lanes; small museums; craft shops.

Uwa Historic quarter (**Seiyo**) – Unomachi street's Meij-era machiya and kura now house sake, soy, kimono and wax shops; museum of folk tools.

Matsuyama backstreets – retro kissaten; second-hand bookshops; everyday city life.

Dogo Onsen (**Matsuyama**) – famous bathhouse precinct; shotengai; nostalgic Iyotetsu tram transportation.

Tobe town (**Matsuyama outskirts**) – home to tobe-yaki, white porcelain brushed with cobalt glaze, many kilns, galleries, workshops.

Historic ports – Imabari's port and temple quarter – maritime shrines to shipbuilding roots, traditional merchant houses; Yawatahama's nostalgic shotengai and markets.

Above: Tensha-en, Uwajima.
Below: Garyu Sanso, Ozu.

MUSEUMS, GALLERIES & CULTURAL LIFE

Ehime Museum of History and Culture (**Seiyu/Ozu**) – prefectural history and vibrant folklore.

The Museum of Art Ehime (**Matsuyama**) – 12,000-plus pieces spanning local and global works.

Imabari Towel Museum – factory, shop and gallery; dedicated to the region's uber-soft cloth.

Ozu Pokopen – Showa-era nostalgia-market and easily overlooked but super-fun mini-museum.

Uchiko-za Kabuki Theatre – active kabuki theatre; centre of the town's cultural revival.

Ikazaki Kite Museum (**Uchiko**) – folk kites, a tradition tied to spring festivals.

Pearl ateliers (**Uwajima**) – exhibitions of pearl culture; links to the coast's long heritage of ama divers.

Creative revival – young makers and preservationists re-energise Uchiko, Ozu and Matsuyama; workshops; cafes; design shops; welcoming vibes.

TRADITIONAL CRAFTS & EXPERIENCES

Imabari towels – Japan's finest towel-making; shopping and chances to see weaving and finishing processes.

Tobe-yaki – kilns and ateliers; cobalt blue tonal glazes; workshops; shopping.

Iyo mizuhiki (**Shikokuchuo**) – traditional paper cords; decorative knot craft; family workshops.

Iyo washi (**Shikokuchuo**) – Kaminochi museum; papermaking workshops (also in Ozu, Uchiko).

Kawara no sato (**Uchiko**) – pottery and paper lamp workshops.

Candlemaking (**Uchiko**) – wax traditions; small studios; living industry.

Soy brewing (**Ozu & Uchiko**) – small-batch shoyu; tastings; brewery visits.

Cultured pearls (**Uwajima**) – hands-on polishing and stringing workshops; pearl farm tours.

Inaka-zushi – country-style sushi classes with local grannies (Seiyo/Uchiko); featuring mountain vegetables, pickles, herbs and sometimes river fish.

Satoyama experiences – foraging; cooking; heritage path walks with farmers; farmstays around Kumakogen, Shingu and Omogo.

FESTIVALS & PERFORMANCE

Summer
Uwajima Ushi-oni Festival (**July**) – bull-demon floats roam the streets; bull sumo contests.

Hotaru Matsuri (**Firefly festival**) (**June**) – Ozu's riverbanks glow with fireflies; popular viewing spot.

Autumn
Saijo Festival (**October**) – danjiri floats; coincides with citrus harvest; farm tours in the hills.

Niihama Taiko Festival (**October**) – giant drums thunder through inland towns; raw energy.

Winter
Dogo Onsen – light-ups; seasonal rituals; all-round warmth in the chilly season.

Omogokei fire festival (**Kumakogen**) (**January**) – pine torches and bonfires purify and protect the valley and climbers; icy rivers and misty gorge lit by fire.

Spring

Ikazaki Kite Festival (**May**) – skies teeming with handpainted fighting kites.

Sakura (**cherry blossoms**) – these crown Matsuyama Castle and park; hanami – blossom-viewing picnics with family and friends.

FOOD & DRINK

Seafood culture – Ehime's coasts yield sea bream (tai), horse mackerel and mackerel; tai meshi (sea-bream rice) honours the succulent fish through Matsuyama's (northern-style) clay-pot rice and Uwajima-style raw tai mixed with soy, rice and egg; bozushi and sabazushi (pressed, bamboo leaf–wrapped sushi); markets remain lively touchstones – Matsuyama's fish market bustles early, while Uwajima's port stalls spill over with the day's catch; jakoten (fried fish cakes) and fukumen (festive noodles with colourful kamaboko and vegetable toppings) bring both flavour and celebration to the table.

Abura-soba (**Ozu**) – aromatic 'oil' dressed noodles.

Yaki-buta tamago-meshi (**Imabari**) – grilled pork and egg over rice.

Iyo Beef – local wagyu with marbling.

Shoyu – sweet, mellow local soy, famously from historic Kajita Shoten brewery.

Above: Ozu's laneways are dotted with local craft shops.
Below: Coming of Age Day photos at Tensha-en.

Yakibuta Tamago-meshi (Imabari) – comfort food; grilled pork, fried egg, sweet soy tare over rice.

Citrus Kingdom – Ehime, the heartland of extraordinary citrus; dozens of varieties grown on coastal terraces; Iyokan, large and aromatic; sweet, gelatinous Beni-madonna; winter's juicy Dekopon; Kawachi Bankan, a crisp-sweet cousin of grapefruit; fruits are found throughout the prefecture in juices, jellies, liqueurs, sweets and ice cream in citrus cafes and stalls.

Sweets – Botchan dango; chestnut confections from inland valleys; bright citrus sweets.

Taruto – sponge roll filled with yuzu scented beanpaste.

Dairy (Hojo) – northern Matsuyama's rich dairy milk and ice cream; mikan milk swirl.

Inaka zushi – mountain side 'country' sushi using pickled vegetables and river fish.

Farmers' produce – seasonal farmhouse dishes; taro; wax gourd; handmade tofu.

Drinks – crisp local sake; citrus liqueurs; craft beer from small breweries.

Cafes and kissaten – retro coffee houses, especially in Matsuyama and Uchiko, popular gathering spots.

Fresh Park Karari – excellent michi-no-eki near Uchiko; casual deck dining by Oda river, under maple trees; local products and delicious citrus gelato.

NATURAL HIGHLIGHTS

The famous 88 Henro – many temples link this section of the spiritual pilgrim's hiking route.

Shimanami Kaido – cycling bridges linking Ehime to Hiroshima above Geiyo islands.

Shikoku Karst (**Kumakogen**) – rolling highland meadows; grazing cows; star gazing; sensational views; cycling; limestone rockfields and basins.

Mount Ishizuchi – Shikoku's highest peak; pilgrim hikes; chain climbs to the summit.

Cape Sada (**Sadamisaki Lighthouse**) – panoramic views from Shikoku's westernmost tip; rustic fishing village; sunset cliffs.

Seaside train – JR Yosan Line clings to the coast between Takamatsu and Uwajima; sea views; photogenic Shimonada platform and sunsets.

Mikan terraces (**Seiyo**) – terraced slopes; orchard lunches; spectacular sea outlook.

Hijikawa River and Valley (**Ozu city and surrounds**) – summer kawadoko platforms; firefly evenings; rice fields; willow trees.

Okudogo hot springs (**Matsuyama**) – rural baths; quieter alternatives to Dogo.

Above: Hijikawa River banks, Ozu.
Below: Uwa Sea views from Karihama, Seiyo.

Kochi (No. 39 – Total cities: 11)

Kochi leans into the Pacific, its coast wide to the horizon and its back turned to mountains thick with yuzu groves around Umaji, ginger terraces and cosmos fields. At its heart, Kochi City is a seaside castle town with the easy camaraderie of a big country community. Markets and Yosakoi dance spill into streets, which clatter with laughter during Tosa no Okyaku parties. Beyond, the Shimanto and Niyodo Rivers run so clear they seem otherworldly, feeding villages, like architecturally famous Yusuhara and Sakawa's historic sake precinct, which remain entwined with nature. This is a prefecture of warmth and unvarnished character – surfboards at dawn, fish grilled at dusk, Tosa-washi pulled in mountain light.

Above: Make your own washi at Kamikoya, Yusuhara.
Opposite: Chikurin-ji (no.31 Henro temple), Kochi city.

REGION 8.

Kyushu & Okinawa

(8 prefectures:
Fukuoka, Saga,
Nagasaki,
Kumamoto,
Oita, Miyazaki,
Kagoshima,
Okinawa)

Fukuoka
(No. 40 – Total cities: 28)

Capping north-western Kyushu, Fukuoka Prefecture exquisitely blends a polished yet relaxed capital city with surrounding fields, canal towns, beaches and hillside hamlets. In the city centre, mornings strolling the paths around Ohori Park give way to nights wandering the Tenjin–Daimyo backstreets. After dark, lantern-lit yatai line the Naka River. Beyond the city, Yame's tea and Kurume's indigo, Ukiha's orchards, Itoshima's sea edge and Yanagawa's boats ground and enrich this lifestyle-driven destination with makers, markets and simple good food.

Above: Forest bathing views over Ukiha's farm terraces.
Below: Sakurai Shrine Futamigaura Torii, Itoshima.

CITIES, TOWNS & VILLAGES

Fukuoka City (capital) – formerly twin towns (Fukuoka and Hakata); this compact, cosmopolitan city boasts an international airport just minutes from its centre, and ferries to Busan; fishmarkets line the shores only steps away from the CBD; bustling shotengai, izakaya, temples, shrines and shopping precincts are fuelled by a thriving coffee culture during daylight hours, and yatai by night. Ohori Park offers a calm, central greenspace.

Dazaifu – Sacred Tenmangu's plum-shaded avenues; raked quiet in Komyozen-ji; umegae mochi grills; a small hill of museums; students wish for exam success, echoing a centuries-old ritual.

Kurume – indigo-dyed kasuri lanes; old-guard ramen counters; small ateliers; evening views from Kora Taisha over the Chikugo Plain; legendary Chikugo River Fireworks draw families for a night of lights and wish-making.

Yame – gyokuro heartland: tea fields; boutique roasters; studio visits; Fukushima's old merchant town; the shrine of Fukushima Hachiman-gu; skilful traditional crafts; paper lantern workshops; stylish homewares; a growing mix of small bars and shops.

Itoshima – slow beaches and farm roads to coastal studios; winter oyster huts; surf coves; sunset cafes; Raizan Sennyo-ji and Sakurai Shrine entwine sea-edge ritual with seasonal spectacle.

Kitakyushu (Moji/Kokura) – Taisho-era Mojiko Retro facades; Tanga Market snacks; castle greens; spring's Kawachi Fujien wisteria tunnel.

Yanagawa – donkobune canal boats; eel kitchens; Tachibana-tei Ohana – a former lord's villa with a garden and museum (and accommodation); white-walled storehouses; boatmen spinning tales of river guardians and kappa water sprites said to lurk under bridges.

Ukiha – 'Fruit kingdom' slopes (persimmon, Amaou strawberries, sweet potato); Yoshii-machi's shirakabe streets; museums; cafes.

Asakura – referred to as Little Kyoto; known for onsen and rotenburo-rich ryokan and Akizuki (meaning autumn moon … swoon), an Edo-period castle town perched in forested hills.

TEMPLES, SHRINES & GARDENS

Kushida-jinja – home to the towering floats of Hakata Gion Yamakasa; prayers for health and protection bind this festival.

Dazaifu Tenmangu, Komyozen-ji (Dazaifu) – spiritual and contemplative centre of Kyushu.

Raizan Sennyo-ji Daihioin (Itoshima) – maple-framed mountain temple, forest trails.

Sakurai Shrine and Futamigaura (Itoshima) – coastal shrine; 'wedded rocks'; giant white torii floating in the sea; wishes for good partnerships.

Miyajidake Shrine (Fukutsu) – the 'Path of Light', when the sun sets straight along the shrine approach in February and October; believed to open fortune's way.

Munakata Taisha – a UNESCO World Heritage–listed triad of sacred shrines honouring sea deities: Hetsu-miya on the mainland, Nakatsu-miya on Oshima and Okitsu-miya on Okinoshima (off-limits, with viewing at Yohaisho); sailors and fishers leave their prayers for safe passage; artefacts and treasure hall.

Nanzoin (**Sasaguri**) – one of the world's largest reclining Buddhas; blessings of health and renewal.

Fukuoka city greenery and calm – Ohori Park; Ohori Park Japanese garden; Rakusuien garden; Yusentei teahouse garden.

Kora Taisha (**Kurume**) – guardian of the regions: grand hilltop shrine overlooking the Chikugo plain.

HISTORIC PRECINCTS

Akizuki (**Asakura**) – delightful castle-town lanes leading to the old gate and the stone Megane Bridge; cafes; impressive ryokan; Seiryuan's exquisite garden; a quietly beautiful maple season.

Yoshii-machi (**Ukiha**) – preserved shirakabe white-walled merchant quarter; riverside laneways; antique shops; historic homes; kura galleries.

Fukuoka Castle ruins (Maizuru Park) – sprawling stone ramparts and moats, springtime plum and cherry blossoms and peonies.

Kokura Castle precinct (**Kitakyushu**) – reconstructed keep; kimono shops; craft studios; tea houses.

Yanagawa canal quarter – willow-lined waterways; boat rides through samurai-era estates.

Kawabata shotengai backstreets (**Fukuoka City**) – tiny shrines; vintage bars; long-standing noodle shops surround the city's oldest shotengai.

Yame Fukushima – gorgeous preserved merchant centre celebrating tea commerce and culture; local crafts; galleries; tearooms; Yamane residence.

MUSEUMS, GALLERIES & CULTURAL LIFE

Fukuoka City

Fukuoka Art Museum – at the edge of Ohori Park; strong modern Japanese and Asian art holdings.

Fukuoka Asian Art Museum – modern and contemporary Asian art; artist in residence programs.

Fukuoka City Museum – local history; trade culture; Momochihama waterfront views; Hakata Traditional Craft and Design Museum (near Kushida-jinja) – features Hakata Ori textiles, Hakata Ningyo dolls; bamboo crafts; demonstrations.

Hakata Machiya Folk Museum (near Kushida-jinja) – Edo-Meiji recreation of town life and craft; hands-on exhibits.

Hakata-za Theatre – grand riverside venue; kabuki; performing arts.

ACROS Fukuoka Step Garden – rooftop terraced greenery; city views; free community art spaces.

Lifestyle hubs (Fukuoka city) – around Tenjin and the Daimyo: Yakuin-Imaizumi grid; creative enclaves; galleries; roaster cafes; boutique design in Kego and Hirao. Hakata Station precinct boasts ramen alleys, izakaya, craft and gourmet shops, a rooftop farm and cultural events. Further west: nostalgic old-world arcades in Nishijin–Fujisaki; Ropponmatsu 421Complex nurtures a growing cultural hub (Tsutaya Books; Fukuoka City Science Museum; rooftop spaces). Weekend flea and handmade markets operate under shrine torii. Bayside warehouses, studios and cafes dot Bayside Place and Chuo Wharf's emerging waterfront scene.

Elsewhere

Yame Traditional Crafts Museum – showcases local crafts like lanterns, bamboo weaving and Buddhist altars; demonstrations, shopping and adjacent michi-no-eki.

Above: Temari craft, Tachibana-tei Ohana.
Below: Contemporary take on tradition at Nakamura Ningyo.

Kurume City Art Museum (**Ishibashi cultural centre**) – Kyushu modernist works; sculpture gardens; Yoga (western-style Japanese paintings).

Kyushu National Museum (**Dazaifu**) – pre-modern Japan–Asia cultural exchange; Kengo Kuma architecture.

Mojiko Grand Market (**Kitakyushu**) – spring and autumn pop-up market in the retro port streets; antiques; craft; food stalls.

TRADITIONAL CRAFTS & EXPERIENCES

Fukuoka city crafts – studio visits; Hakata-ningyo doll painting; Hakata-ori coaster weaving; bamboo craft; ramen broth or gyoza class with a local chef.

Kurume-kasuri weaving and indigo dyeing (**Kurume**) – textile shops and demonstrations; hands-on experiences.

Tea craft (**Yame**) – picking; hand rolling; blending; roasting; tea ceremony experiences.

Lanterns (**Yame**) – paper lantern workshop.

Pottery – Koishiwara-yaki (Toho Village); Takatori-yaki (Tagawa/Soeda); Agano-yaki (Fukuchi).

Markets and food walks – guided tastings at Yanagibashi Rengo Market; Nagahama Fish Market open days and canteen breakfast; yatai routes with a local.

Eel culture (**Yanagawa**) – preparation and cookery demonstrations.

Ukiha fruit picking – mingle with farmers and locals in one of Japan's most fertile fruitbowls.

Itoshima makers – pottery; woodwork; weekend pop-ups.

FESTIVALS & PERFORMANCE

Summer
Hakata Gion Yamakasa (**July**) – pre-dawn race; water-throwing; born from plague-averting rituals.

Tobata Gion Oyamagasa (**Kitakyushu, July**) – lanternlit floats carrying the pulse of a port town.

Chikugo River Fireworks (**Kurume, August**) – one of western Japan's largest and oldest displays (founded 1650); 18,000 fireworks set at separate riverbanks, yukatas worn; picnics.

Autumn
Hakozaki-gu Hojo-ya (**September**) – harvest rites; craft fairs; shrine festivals.

Winter
Kyushu Basho (**November**) – grand sumo tournament; some stables open early-morning practice (asageiko) to quiet observers.

Hakushu Festival (**Yanagawa, November**) – lantern-lit canal boats pay tribute to poet and lyricist Kitahara Hakushu; quiet; local.

Spring
Plum blossom at Dazaifu – heralds the start of spring; perfuming shrine precincts.

Kawachi Fujien (**Kitakyushu**) (**late April–May**) – stroll through dreamy wisteria tunnels.

Hakata Dontaku Port Festival in Golden Week (**May**) – waterfront dance parades; drums; flower-decked boats.

Yanagawa Sagemon (**February–April**) – local Hina (doll) festival; riverside homes and canal boats glow with good-luck ornaments, including handmade silk temari balls.

Above: Cafe life, Odori Park.
Below: Eel cuisine, Yanagawa.

FOOD & DRINK

Local specialties – Fukuoka's famous Tonkotsu (rich pork broth) ramen and Kurume ramen (both originated in Kurume); gyoza (including the tetsunabe iron-pan style); yatai nights (Nakasu/Naka River and city clusters); mentaiko; mizutaki chicken hot pot; motsunabe and horumonyaki (offal – hotpots and grilled); Kayanoya dashi tastings; coastal seafood; goma-saba (sesame mackerel); gobo-ten (fried burdock) often paired with soft Hakata udon; Unagi no seiryo mushi – Yanagawa's steamed and sweetly glazed eel over rice; Itoshima kakigoya (oyster shacks) (winter only); Asakura's majestic Persimmon, Pears and Amaou strawberries (Ukiha/Asakura); umegae mochi (Dazaifu).

Markets and Michi-no-Eki – Yanagibashi Rengo Market (Fukuoka city's 'kitchen'); Nagahama Fish market, Itoshima JA markets; Michi-no-Eki Ito Saisai (Itoshima); Ukiha fruit roadside stations (some offer pick your own).

Drinks – Chikugo's Jojima district sake breweries; Yame tea fields, gyokuro/matcha; third-wave coffee; shochu bars.

Ryokan and kaiseki – Dazaifu, Asakura and Yanagawa inns; Yame countryside inns with tea-focused menus; Itoshima coastal stays.

Rail dining experiences – gourmet carriages on THE RAIL KITCHEN CHIKUGO showcasing Chikugo produce; luxury Seven Stars in Kyushu, which begins and ends in Hakata station with multi-course seasonal menus.

NATURAL HIGHLIGHTS

Walk, hike, cycle – Itoshima capes, beaches and Shiraito Falls; Shikanoshima causeway scenic cycle loop; Dazaifu forest paths and Mount Homan hikes; seasonal wisteria walks in Kitakyushu; Sasaguri mini-pilgrimage linking Nanzoin with forest chapels; Aburayama Citizens' Forest walks.

Life aquatic – canal cruising in Yanagawa; surfing in Itoshima; Keya no Oto sea cave boats (Itoshima); Momochi Seaside Park and Fukuoka Tower sunset; rowboats on Ohori Park lake; Naka River evening cruises past yatai; Hakata Bay water bus and sunset boats; ferry to Nokonoshima flower park and Uminonakamichi Seaside Park.

Saga (No. 41 – Total cities: 10)

Saga is felt in distinctive, time-slowing moments: fisherfolk calling across Yobuko's morning market, squid glistening in their hands; kilns glowing in secluded valleys and misted hillsides where ateliers double as homes and monkeys chatter from the rooftops; farmhouse hospitality; Nijinomatsubara pines dancing over wind-cut Karatsu Bay; moonlit reflections in Hamanoura rice terraces. The prized porcelain towns of Imari and Arita lend an elegant edge. In Karatsu's castle town and tea-centric Ureshino's onsen valley, younger generations reshape old spaces – coffee roasters occupy merchant houses, izakaya line retro yokocho and brewery streets hum with live DJs.

Nagasaki (No. 42 – Total cities: 13)

Nagasaki Prefecture reclines along Kyushu's west coast between harbourside hills and island-scattered seas. The capital's Peace Park champions reflection. Chinatown and the intricately restored Dejima recall early exchange. Offshore, the Goto Islands drift on the East China Sea, and their villages are shaped by the still operating camellia oil industry and centuries-old Christian influences. Inland, Unzen's volcanic plateau rewards hikers with hot springs and sweeping views. Obama's seaside foot baths and Shimabara's koi-filled canals nod to the region's relaxed, playful side.

Sueyama (aka Tozan) shrine's striking Arita-ware ceramic Torii gate, Saga.

Kumamoto (No. 43 – Total cities: 14)

In the shadow of Mount Aso, Kumamoto's fertile valleys are shaped by fire and ash. The prefecture's bold character shows in its black castle walls, Aso's smouldering rim, raucous autumn horse parades, spicy karashi renkon and unshakable warmth.

Puppet plays endure in mountain hamlets. Amakusa's chapels recall once-forbidden faith. Itsuki's forests cradle haunting lullabies. On the swift Kuma River, kayakers chase rapids where dragons are said to stir, and clear waters give rise to revered Kuma shochu.

Oita (No. 44 – Total cities: 14)

Oita urges travellers to relax and restore. In Beppu, vents hiss from the gutters, where steam from boiling jigoku (hells) cooks meals and warms onsen towns. At Usa Jingu, Shinto and Buddhism converge beneath ancient cedars. In Kitsuki, ghosts of samurai and merchants share the streets. Misty Yufuin hosts galleries and small inns. Onta-yaki pots are shaped by river power, shiitake fatten in oak groves, yuzu-kosho sharpens local fare and barley shochu drinks light and clean – a taste of the land's true spirit.

Miyazaki (No. 45 – Total cities: 9)

The sunshine prefecture, Miyazaki, stretches along Kyushu's Pacific coast with subtropical ease. Nichinan's palm-lined shores, citrus groves and Hyuga's breezy breaks carry an undercurrent of creation myths

Above: Kitzuki castle town.
Below: Nearby Futago-ji's lush temple grounds, Oita.

that shape an innate generosity locals call 'hinata' (the sunny side of life). Amaterasu is worshipped at Aoshima Shrine. In Takachiho, kagura chants and drumbeats reverberate through mountain halls near the Ama-no-Iwato cave, where Amaterasu once retreated.

Kagoshima (No. 46 – Total cities: 19)

In Kyushu's south, Kagoshima looks across a wide bay to the smoking silhouette of Sakurajima. Satsuma heritage lies close to the surface here – gardens cut with stone, black vinegar jars fermenting in the sun, kiriko glass that morphs into art, and cuisine built around rich Kurobuta (black pigs). Trams and ferries tie the relaxed capital to onsen towns, teahouses, winter crane fields and far-off islands. In summer, locals enjoy shaved ice sluiced with citrus or spiked with imo shochu as sea light refracts over black sand beaches.

Okinawa (No. 47 – Total Cities: 11)

Officially Region 8 (Kyushu and Okinawa), but treated separately in tourism contexts due to its distinct island culture and geography. Okinawa rolls at its own pace – a subtropical chain shaped by centuries of Ryukyu trade, layered with history and softened by island time. Coral seas, subtropical forests and stone-walled villages frame a culture where shisa lions guard rooftops and sanshin music spills into the night. Influences from China, Southeast Asia and wider Japan drift through Okinawan food, textiles and rituals, yet the flavour is entirely its own. Tropical and timeless.

Above: Shisa guardians on Taketomi Island rooftops.
Below: Ishigaki Island's photogenic Kabira Bay.

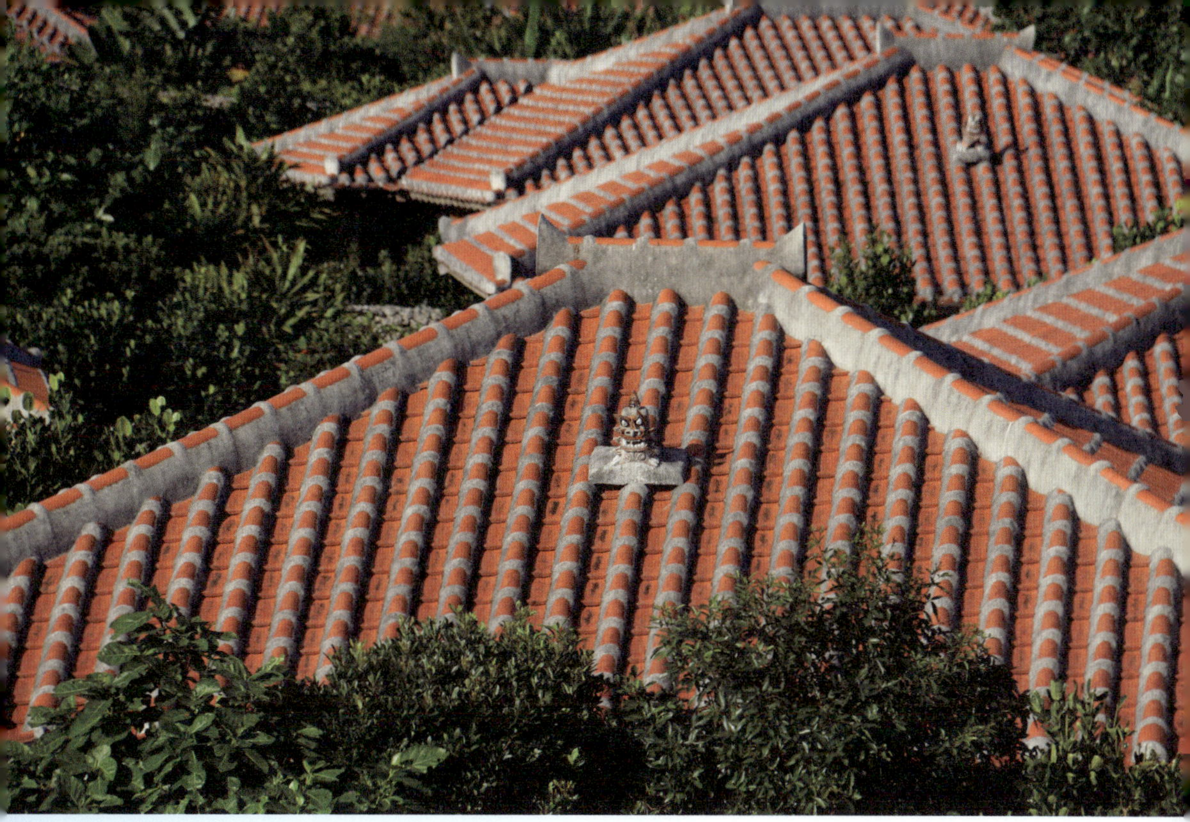
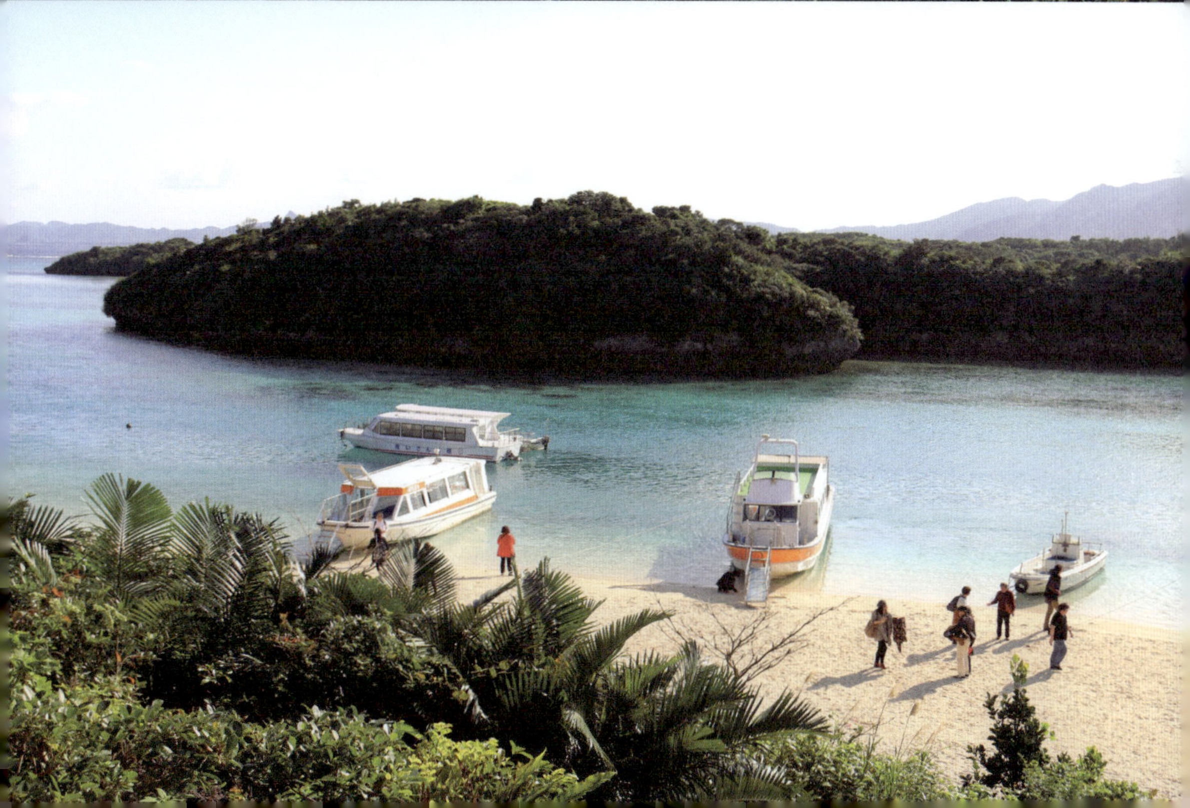

Tips on Exploring the Prefectures and Regions

▶ As your interest is sparked, loop an invisible and flexible boundary around your selected prefectures or regions by plotting them on a personalised online map (such as Google My Maps). You'll soon find yourself inside an enjoyable bubble of intrigue leading you to authentic, personalised itinerary development.

▶ Investigate places or items you find appealing within each bubble. You'll be further rewarded with unanticipated additional options, providing rare insight into true local life and culture that you won't find elsewhere. You'll also quickly determine the distance between destinations of interest, which will instantly suggest which adjacent regions might be worth exploring.

▶ As you plunge deeper, you'll discover information you may not have sought, but which offers more than you'd hoped for. Let this inspire you to devise an itinerary based on a theme of your choosing – for example, pottery or textiles, architecture or design, gardens, temples, Edo-period towns, onsen villages, hikes, cycle trails, natural wonders, technology, poetry or tea. Perhaps you'll plot a ramen pilgrimage, or mountain-village-hop along a single train line without agenda. At the same time, your preferred style of travelling Japan may become evident as you locate unique accommodation options or transport methods. You might discover your travel preferences are subconsciously led by things of a spiritual, historic, cultural, adventurous, foodie or artful nature – which may in turn trigger

an exploration of areas you'd never dreamt would call for a closer look.

▶ Create your own searchable map legend by using the icons, symbols and colourisation features on My Maps. This will also make points of interest easy to recognise. Maintain one 'hero' My Map, adding everything that grabs you – then, when you're ready to plan a specific trip, copy and paste a relevant selection of places over to a fresh My Map. There, you can add personal notes, directions and planned routes with key stops en route. Don't forget to allow free time for serendipity. You can add things you find as you go and wish to return to, or share your map with a friend so they can follow your travels and furnish the map with their favourite places, too. Don't forget to create pins from the various mentions and recommendations heavily threaded throughout this book.

▶ Word endings provide clues to the nature of a site; generally -ji, -do, -dera or -in at the end of a word indicates a temple (Kiyomizu-dera, Senso-ji). Shrine names end in -jinja, -jingu, -taisha or -gu (Kitano Tenman-gu, Yasaka-jinja). Similarly, -en announces a garden or park, -sanso is a villa, -rikyu is an imperial villa and -jo is a castle.

▶ This kind of travel planning offers a more textural and melodious journey, yielding a layered and lasting understanding of place and people. Notice how culture differs from region to region. You cannot easily recognise what's distinctive and extraordinary about each without taking the time to get to know them. Once you've travelled this way, you won't look back.

Seasoning
– Deciding When to Travel

I woke at 3.05am gasping for air. My sheets were soaked; my body on fire. I felt certain my expiry date had arrived. Fuzzy-headed and weak, I somehow managed to inhale the jug of water that lived beside my bed before noticing my partner crouched over me with wide eyes – clearly sharing the suspicion of my fate. The night before, we'd installed a nifty cool mat – an insulated foil sheet that claimed to prevent your body temperature from rising to an uncomfortable level. My error in not having translated the small print was more than unfortunate – on closer reading, I discovered that if the room temperature remained below 30°C I was good to go, but once the temperature increased, so would the mat's heat – and onwards it would rise.

Sunset at Shimabara, overlooking the Ariake Sea, Nagasaki Prefecture.

'All we need is some olive oil and rosemary to baste you with,' my partner joked. This was not the concerned and caring check-in I was seeking from my love. Our temporary home was a 60s concrete block, originally built as public housing. It was thankfully larger than other apartments I'd lived in, but it lacked air conditioning or anything resembling a breeze – unless the front door and back windows were wide open at precisely 3pm, and even then, anything even masquerading as relief was fleeting.

We were thrilled to discover another stellar cooling apparatus – a steering wheel-shaped gel pack devised to be frozen then fitted across the face of a standing electric fan, where it was meant to direct an icy blast over our roasting bodies. I woke, again in the hottest part of the evening, to find the fan's base sitting in a pool of water, just waiting to cook us by an alternative method. And so it continued, sleep seemingly unattainable.

We eventually sought solace at a friend's shack on the shore of Biwa-ko, Japan's largest freshwater lake.

'Come relax in the shade,' they said.

'Bring your swimmers,' they enthused – and it sounded like the perfect antidote to the heat.

On arrival, we tumbled into a beautifully green and shady but overgrown tangle of garden. We were greeted by a small, venomous snake and an excited foreign lad known as Reptile Boy, whose encyclopaedic knowledge of the slithery vertebrates was impressive, but not in the least reassuring. My nerves, far past the point of being frazzled by that stage, impressively leapt to attention when someone suggested a swim. I shuffle-hopped my bare feet over the scorching, dark sand, body and mind aching for refreshment. I plunged myself into the promise of relief.

Instead, I found myself soaking in a steaming broth of dead frogs and neatly chomped watermelon rinds. Our simmering surrounds were laced with motor oil, which seeped from the mosquito-pitched dinghies being raced nearby by peroxided revheads – seemingly unaware of the rest of the otherwise unoccupied lake, which has a circumference of almost 240 kilometres. I was assured it's much cleaner in other parts, particularly those further away from train tracks and roads. I hoped so, given the lake is a famous breeding ground for ayu (sweet fish) – a 'delicacy' in the cooler months, commonly cooked over a grill.

Back home, covered in a mix of sweat, oily residue and the natural exfoliant of grit mixed with fine dust, I threw off my clothes, gagging to rinse off in a cool shower. However, by the time the antiquated water pipes reached my bathroom on the sixth floor, the 'cold' water was running at the same temperature as the rest of the apartment that balmy evening – around 40°C.

In desperation, I slumped my overheated body into the foetal position on the tiles, allowing the water to trickle over me as I attempted to trick my brain by thinking cool thoughts to reduce the discomfort – a skill the Japanese have mastered. For example, one might purposely walk through a calming, shady forest of towering green bamboo. Despite the humidity and heat that stews inside those steamy jade tunnels, mind-over-matter coerces respite. On this occasion, however, my inner strength was spent, and I was utterly overwhelmed. The bathroom felt as though a gremlin had switched on non-existent underfloor heating.

To survive the remainder of the summer, I avoided being outside in daylight as much as possible because each step felt like wading through armpit-high mud; the heaviness of the atmosphere made each breath feel like I was under water. When I dared to venture out, I skipped the sweltering bus, opting instead for air-conditioned taxis to the nearest department store or movie theatre, where I'd linger to temporarily lower my otherwise unrelenting 'fever'.

I could not sufficiently hydrate no matter how much H$_2$O I guzzled. I stocked up on soft drink from the ground-floor supermarket and drowned my insides with sugar, but any energy it provided was fleeting.

Eventually it occurred to me that the sports drink Pocari Sweat was not just restricted to post-workout consumption, and that there was method behind the madness of the recently landed seasonal soft drink range that read like a pickle-shop menu – think salted lychee or watermelon, or enhanced waters infused with tomato, shiso or cucumber. The reason for the 'stamina-recipe' mooks piled high at supermarket checkouts also became clear – they were not dishes to cook for sumo wrestlers, as I'd assumed, but foods your body requires to prevent the kind of heat exhaustion and dehydration that I would later be diagnosed with.

Perhaps I should have picked up on earlier cues. We were staying in this Kyoto apartment thanks to the generosity of friends who chose to annually escape the extremities of summer by exiting the country.

Winter presented another extreme. We were thrilled to be house-sitting our mates' charmingly rustic timber home in the mountains surrounding Kyoto, until we found that it was literally freezing indoors, day and night. The Japanese are always quick to point out that traditional homes are built with summers and earthquakes in mind, the wooden structures allowing excellent airflow and flexibility. However, I remain perplexed about the lack of winter planning in a country that receives at least a smattering of snow in most places. Historically, people both kept warm and cooked food over an irori (hearth) or charcoal-filled vessels. This is a messy, time-consuming business, so eventually a survival kit of kerosene-fuelled heaters, electric blankets and rugs, and kotatsu (low tables covered with quilted electric blankets meant for getting cosy, and sometimes for napping) became the norm.

Despite the fumes, kerosene lamps are a reasonably priced and effective way to eliminate the cold, and it can be kind of romantic, if you choose to see it that way … until you catch the flu. One evening, as my fever escalated and the outside temperatures dropped, condensation cascaded down the windows and walls. By the wee hours, ice crystals had crawled across each internal windowpane, forming frosty curtains that refused to melt until peak sunlight the next day, when they would eventually form puddles on the tatami. This freeze-and-defrost cycle continued for several days, chilling us through to our bone marrow. My bladder betrayed me again and again. I spent the darkest, coldest hours crab-walking my cumbersome gaijin (foreigner) feet up and down the steep, age-polished, shallow stairwells, clutching the walls for dear life, steadying myself for the icy sting of the porcelain squat toilet.

While the former inhabitants of this old house would have washed and soaked at the local sento (bathhouse), we had the dubious privilege of a modern adaptation: a small, deep bath located in a corner of the tiny, frigid kitchen. No matter how I tried, sustaining my body warmth during the transition from bath to my thermals was impossible. No amount of Nikka Whisky From the Barrel or ginger-spiked chicken ramen was going to help. The flu came for me. At the height of my malaise, I vaguely remember rousing my husband with a wing to the ribs, warning him of monkeys clambering over the roof … they'd soon be entering through the windows to eat my face off, I told him. I know for a fact that they can slide the windows open in that very house, so I am not completely deranged – but the rest, I'll admit, was the fever speaking. And possibly the whisky.

Lake Biwa tori (bird) on on Torii (shrine gate) at Shirahige-jinja, Shiga Prefecture.

My purpose in sharing the stories above is not to highlight my prowess for whining about the weather. Rather it's to initially demonstrate how unfavourable information is often omitted around seasonal travel depending on who's doing the reporting – certain aspects potentially take a toll on your body or spirit once you step away from your air-conditioned hotel room. So, seasonal considerations are handy to know about and prepare for.

Unless dictated by employment or set holidays, when to travel is generally a personal choice and in deciding the best time for a trip, people do commonly look to the seasons. It might not have been obvious from the stories I've just shared, but I am a winter gal through and through – it suits me better to travel in the colder months for a range of personal reasons, none of them involving skiing. However, I wouldn't have given up one minute of my worst moments in the most scorching Japanese summers, or hideously crowded sakura (cherry blossom) or koyo (autumn leaves) seasons – because they've helped shape my Japan story in a way that would not be possible if I had stayed within my comfort zone, honouring my predilection towards winter travel. The brief periods of discontent have far been outweighed – enriched, even – by the quirks and gifts of each season. Clearly, these moments have stayed with me. They're difficult to forget, really. At the end of the day, follow what you know works for you physically and mentally – or, alternatively, trust your ability to make the most of an inclement situation, even if it doesn't suit you.

Located in the northern hemisphere, Japan's long stretch of islands sees temperatures warming the country from its toes in tropical and subtropical southern regions through to its humid continental far north, and it cools down in reverse.

Spring, for example, arrives earlier in the southern Japanese islands. The iconic sakura (cherry blossoms) shimmy up a show as early as January in Okinawa, before popping up on the furthest tip of Japan's northernmost island, Hokkaido, where these tiny beauties may not fully bloom until June. On the flipside, autumn arrives first in Hokkaido, with leaves starting to turn by mid– to late October, the cooler weather having crept in from September. The Kansai region in south-west Honshu waits until mid-November to early December for the same, while southern island Kyushu holds out until mid-December for its showing of autumn colour.

No matter where you travel in Japan, you may notice weather anomalies and a variety of microclimates. These are caused by several factors, one of them being an 80 per cent mountainous landscape with pockets of extremely high-density living. We all know that taking general weather reports as gospel can set you up for disappointment. In Japan in particular, it can be beneficial to drill down into *very* local weather information. This will give you a truer reading that might be relevant to your travel needs, including when particular flowers bloom (see p. 175), or leaves turn, or the snow starts or the rainy season arrives – which may be entirely different in the closest larger city.

You can freely find a mix of information online about average temperatures, rainfall, forecasted blooms, pollen levels, fog, smog and the most active typhoon periods, as well as what to expect or how to dress appropriately during each period. However, there are always other pros and cons surrounding when to travel, and it's certainly helpful to be informed on more than the weather.

Discounting Golden Week (an extended string of public holidays in early May), the two most popular travel periods for both Japanese and international tourists are peak spring and autumn – both of which are undeniably beautiful, but can also be maddening. Winter is phenomenally busy at the more popular ski resorts, usually swarming with Australians thrilled by the proximity of incredible powder snow at the same time as their southern hemisphere summer.

Peak periods attract premium pricing. With essentials like flights and accommodation being considerably more expensive at such times, it's surprising more travellers aren't deterred. Additionally, there are eternal queues, hotels at capacity, overflowing restaurants and public transport, certain loud and disrespectful foreigners and lack of personal space – all of which can make travel (and life for locals) extremely unpleasant.

I have always preferred to travel during off-peak seasons, which are (in my opinion) the best times to visit Japan. It's quieter – you can sit on a temple deck or park bench, by a riverside or alpine field and process your thoughts. You're free to wander through gardens, museums, galleries and cultural precincts soaking up the atmosphere without being trampled. As the country's popularity continues to soar, there are fewer of those delicious moments readily available in more famous regions – but seek them out, and you will find them. Again, it's about learning where and how by searching further afield. Moreso, it's about making the most of whenever and wherever you visit – simply shifting your focus around that can have impactful results.

Meeting sekki and ko – good things come in small packages

In the early Meiji era (1868–1912), Japan adopted the Gregorian calendar, aligning more closely with Western seasonal divisions. Previously the Japanese observed the lunisolar calendar, which divided the year into 24 semi-seasons of roughly 15 days duration, known as sekki, inherited from China's seasonal flow. Due to nature and climate inconsistencies between the two lands, and therefore the growth cycles of plants and animals, sekki were further refined by the Japanese into 72 microseasons, or ko (kou), each lasting roughly five days. Every ko is bestowed with an evocative title such as 'north wind blows the leaves from the trees', 'crickets chirp around the door', 'wild geese return' and 'first peach blossoms', noting subtle changes in the weather, atmosphere and environment.

Japan's native Shinto religion values an intimate reverence for nature. Harmony and purity are sought through worshipping the kami (sacred spirits or divine presences), which inhabit all naturally occurring things – living organisms such as plants and animals as well as inanimate objects such as rocks, mountains, rain and thunder, the moon and sun. Ancestors are also venerated as spirit guardians, reflecting the enduring connection between the living and the dead in Japanese belief (see p. 179).

Some farmers, hunters or fisherfolk still follow the microseasons. Even among city dwellers, it's not uncommon to be aware of when a particular flower blooms, even if it's for a single day, or to await a sansai (mountain vegetable) bud's arrival at the local market, perfect for tempura before its natural bitterness sets in. Over that tight handful of days, there will be a queue to snap them up before they disappear for another year.

Even though sekki and ko have specific date periods attached, unexpected weather events and changes in the climate obviously affect the actual dates of occurrence. Nevertheless, the ancient way provides an engaging and poetic guide to the cyclic order of things. Observing them strips back all the noise, allowing one to slow down enough to appreciate moments in time that might otherwise be taken for granted.

Twelve months in Japan – a seasonal snapshot

Please remember that while actual timings are dependent on climate anomalies, generally spring flowers and summers arrive a couple of months later in northern Japan, while autumn leaves and winter arrive earlier, and vice versa for southern Japan.

WINTER: DECEMBER, JANUARY, FEBRUARY

Japan transitions from the end of the old year into the start of the new during a period which traditionally embodies a sense of reflection, quiet celebration and serenity. Early December, in many parts, offers chilly yet often clear blue skies, providing the perfect backdrop for leisurely walks, whether it's temple-hopping, shopping or hiking before the ice sets in. However, temperatures drop significantly in northern Japan, and the ski season officially kicks off across most resorts by mid-December. While you may be aware of Japan's key winter resorts, there are many wonderful places to consider skiing outside these regions. Some are great for beginners or families – for example, you could check out those in and near Nikko's Yumoto Onsen, Gifu's Gujo or Fukui's Katsuyama. For those seeking more tranquil snowscapes, there are plenty of picturesque villages found in rural areas throughout the country – try Gifu's Takayama (see p. 93) and Shirakawa-go (see p. 93); Kyoto's Miyama (see p. 101) and Ohara (see p. 101); and Nagano's Togakushi or Narai-juku (see p. 93) to start.

Friends and families rug up for 'Kurisumasu' illuminations and markets, while young lovers borrow Christmas Eve for a romantic date night, akin to Valentine's Day. On 25 December, while not a holiday, families commonly pre-order special KFC meals to share, followed by cream-covered strawberry shortcake – note the

commonality of red and white, the auspicious colours of Japan's flag, setting the theme for a celebration indirectly influenced by America's occupation, affluence and the culture Japan was exposed to during and post-World War II. By December's end, folks begin to cull, clear and clean residences and businesses, freeing up space and energy for o-shogatsu festivities (see p. 108). As the cooler evenings set in, the focus shifts to savouring the decadence of winter seafood, and *nabe* (hot pot) dining (see p. 224) comes to the fore, providing a comforting and communal dining experience.

In late December and early January, a very different New Year is observed and much of Japan hangs out the 'back soon' sign until around 7–10 January. During this important period, people commonly return to the regions to visit relatives, habitually causing kisei rasshu (homecoming rush) and mass exodus from larger cities. Temperatures continue to drop throughout January, reaching winter's peak in early February when plums blossom – in the weeks that follow, the land slowly starts to thaw. Restorative onsen beckon and northern ski fields jump!

There's also plenty of bookshop, museum and gallery browsing to be done, as well as lingering coffee stops and crafting workshops (see p. 252), not to mention rugged-up strolls in stark winter gardens (see p. 186). Early February's festival of Setsubun casts out evil spirits to cries of 'fuku wa uchi, oni wa soto!' – inviting 'in' good fortune. This period also features stunning snow festivals in Hokkaido (Sapporo and Asahikawa) featuring enormous yet intricate snow and ice sculptures.

SPRING: MARCH, APRIL, MAY

Crisp, new spring days mark the beginning of renewed life, and people's excitement for outdoor activities increases. Buds (both edible and ornamental) embrace the warmth of the sun, fuelling conversations about culinary and scenic endeavours. Young vegetables are honoured on tempura and kaiseki menus Japan-wide. Sakura (cherry blossom) season ramps up from late March to early April. A bizarrely well-kept secret (or perhaps it's just a mostly ignored memo) is that you can enjoy the cherry blossoms in a highly pleasant and relaxed manner, sometimes without bumping into another soul, simply by shifting your timing or direction slightly (see p. 176). The same applies for autumn's peak.

What's the catch? There isn't one. Cherry blossoms (and stunning autumnal hues) exist across the length and breadth of the country every year with region-dependent timing variations. This means there's no reason to be 'packed like sushi rice' in the parks and gardens of well-known cities.

The incredibly famous sakura (cherry blossoms) and autumn's maple leaves are not the only distinctive seasonal beauties on display across Japan. If that comes as a surprise, it demonstrates how easily we lean into tourism publicity shots and blurbs. Of course, Japan is not alone in this, but focusing promotion on the things or regions that tourism bodies *think* will interest foreigners because they're familiar or recognisable is, as I see it, one of the drivers of over-tourism in parts of Japan. It is also to the detriment of other regions, who risk non-existence without visitation.

The sakura's magnificent, endemic bloom is fragile and fleeting. It lasts only a week or so; less in wind and rain. It has come to symbolise elegance, impermanence and renewal – tying into the central Buddhist concept of the eternal circle of life and death. Sakura have long been associated with samurai, who often led brief but colourful lives and were strong fans of tea ceremonies (see p. 247) – an opportunity to 'be in the moment', ever so briefly removed from the atrocities of the battlefield.

Sakura's arrival officially launches spring – at least on the Western calendar. However, Japan also nods to the old lunar calendar as is situationally appropriate, where spring is also recognised around Setsubun (3 or 4 February), sometimes coinciding with the timing of Chinese New Year. Hanami (a celebratory flower-viewing festival) runs right across Japan during peak sakura season, with times fluctuating within the regions (and yes, I am repeating this fact for emphasis). This harmonious social gathering commonly involves picnicking on a sea of blue tarps beneath fulsome blooms (honouring the rice kami who are believed to inhabit cherry trees), often accompanied by free-flowing nihonshu (sake).

In charming Hakodate city, at the foot of Hokkaido, the cherry trees surrounding Goryokaku's star-shaped fort bloom around mid to late April. Further north, you'll find them exploding all over Sapporo's Odori Park from late April to early May. Still further north, you're looking at mid to late May and sometimes early June. In southernmost Japan, Okinawa for example, the blossoms burst as early as January. Around warmer land fringes and cooler, high-altitude inland peaks, and with microclimates added to the mix, dates can coincide with locations further north or south, rather than those dictated by their immediate surrounds. While this is a little confusing, it's one of the many reasons to drill down into a region's specific offerings when considering your travel plans.

Festivities and activities stir as the air currents warm. In eastern Shikoku's Kochi Prefecture, where spring sets in a little earlier than Honshu, sake-fuelled street picnics are in full swing here by mid-March for the Tosa no Okyaku festival. In other regions, spring festivals like the alpine Takayama's Sanno Matsuri must remain patient until mid-April. The end of April until around 5 May sees most of Japan taking advantage of a stretch of national holidays

---

Weeping Sakura snows petals in the breeze.

referred to as 'Golden Week', which brings many towns and villages to capacity. Golden Week dates change annually, so check before you book any travel during this period.

Many, but not all, mountain regions are thawed enough for hiking by mid-May. Elsewhere, the entire month experiences a domino effect of spectacular florals (see p. 182) including wisteria, azaleas, peonies, roses and the mighty iris. Parks and gardens are awash with colour and admirers. By the month's end, there's a last push of lush greenery and foliage in preparation for the summer shade. Baby lime ginkgo leaves act as tiny fans, while feathery willow leaf hangings block angular sun rays, lulling one into a false sense of cool as they sway hypnotically in the gentlest breeze.

SUMMER: JUNE, JULY, AUGUST

Significant rainfall (aka the rainy season) announces the start of summer and humidity arrives by the bucketload in June, making it the perfect time to seek shelter in abundant indoor art galleries, cultural facilities and excellent shopping precincts. Kabuki (see p. 258) season also kicks off in June with month-long performance programs

found at Japan's three eminent kabuki theatres: Tokyo's Kabuki-za, Osaka's Shochikuza and Kyoto's Minamiza.

Socialising ramps up in the evenings, aided by the seasonal boom of outdoor concerts, festivals, fireworks and rooftop-to-riverside beer garden pop-ups. Summer is the only time of the year you'll find city folk whipping off stockings and socks to dangle their feet in rivers, while kids hop and splash over stepping stones attempting to cool off.

Obon is a major summer event observed nationwide to honour the spirits of ancestors and typically celebrated while holidaying with family. It's among many summer festivals that honour deities who offer protection and luck. Frosty drinks, overtly sweet and lurid kakigori (a cheap version of the sublime shaved ice sweet – see p. 236), chilled cucumbers on sticks and other refreshments, as well as the donning of lightweight cotton yukata (summer kimono) in the streets are all part of these cultural events. Live outdoor music events draw huge local crowds (see p. 258) and outdoor dining increases at night.

Along Kyoto's Kamogawa river and those of Kibune and Takao in northern Kyoto, dining platforms (kawayuka or kawadoko) are laid out, desperately summoning a cool breeze that rarely responds, the pleasing music of running water providing the most 'cooling' aspect, if you can ignore the mosquito hum.

AUTUMN (FALL): SEPTEMBER, OCTOBER, NOVEMBER

Humidity slowly starts to wane, but the heat often lingers well into October. Typhoon season adds to the mix from around September, pointing towards a few indoor days. Preparations are made for the traditional harvest period when special moon-viewing events and related festivals rise to the occasion (see p. 108). By mid-November, a detectable chill signals the turning of the leaves, which persists into December, forming the most divine patchwork of autumn colour across the country. Popular areas and sites swarm with camera-toting tourists, and access to facilities and entertainment can be limited as everything fills or books out quickly. Temples and their gardens in major cities can become very crowded – including night-time light-ups of the momiji (maple trees).

Momiji is to autumn as sakura is to spring. Translating as 'Japanese maple', but with the kanji also reading as 'red leaf', the word 'momiji' is often used as a general term for the autumn leaves. Japanese maples are the most famous trees in the leaf carnival and momiji-gari (maple-leaf hunting) is common practice. It's also hard to ignore ginkgo (ichou), which changes from almost fluorescent green young leaves in summer to darker green and a buttery gold at the end of their cycle, when they fall to create a carpet of sunshine, often left alone to enhance the atmosphere of the season. Momiji-bafu (liquid amber – the name says it all) also springs to mind when I think of koyo (the formal term for 'autumn leaves') in Japan. Fallen leaves (rakuyou) are often repurposed as natural compost, left in gardens to enrich the soil. Leaves are also used in seasonal rituals, symbolising the beauty of impermanence. If you're familiar with the term 'wabi-sabi' (the comprehension of beauty in imperfection, often caused by age, weathering or happenstance damage), then you'll appreciate this gesture. If you'd like to learn more, check out a neat little book by the name of *Wabi-Sabi for Artists, Designers, Poets and Philosophers* by Leonard Koren. Like most things in Japan, the concept is less defined and more obscure than words can well describe, offering 'ma' or empty space for pondering the concept.

Leaf peepers will be blown away by an autumn spent in any part of Japan, and moving away from central Japan to do this guarantees a less crowded experience. Special seasonal train journeys and boat

rides are employed for the purpose of koyo viewing, as they are often in spring's peak blossom season. Trust me, if you don't dig things too 'peopley', all are more pleasant to enjoy in lesser-known regions.

Autumnal hiking increases in popularity as the temperatures cool in mid to late November, particularly in southern islands of Shikoku (popular is the Henro 88, a pilgrimage visiting 88 temples) and Kyushu – think prefectural Fukuoka, Oita, Miyazaki's Takahicho Gorge, Kagoshima and Yakushima Island. The end of autumn, with its crisp, sunshiny weather, is wonderful for contemplative wandering, absorbing the energy of change – a final flurry of movement before winter arrives to slow things down, and the cycle begins anew.

The language of flowers

Returning from day-tripping through the amber-cloaked mountains of Shikoku's Kochi Prefecture one autumn day, my tour guests and I happened upon an enormous field of candy pink cosmos by the side of the road. Without protective fences, these attention-seeking blooms called us over to play. Communal gasping from the group prompted our bus driver to do something most unusual – he stepped out of his comfort zone to suggest an unscheduled stop. He didn't need to ask twice.

Six mature women, carefully assisted by our keen driver, hopped out with cameras at the ready. Initially, we respectfully snapped away from the edge of the field – not daring to advance after learning it was a commercial flower farm. However, as no-one else seemed bothered about intruding, some took a few tentative steps into the blushing pink. Others got down low, face to face with the pretty petals, attempting to capture the essence of their joy, breathing in the moment. Lingering. The intoxicating scene felt like a gift waiting to be unwrapped – a sentiment clearly shared by

the young families who roamed the rows, pushing prams with one hand, leading the elderly by the other. Glamorous female friendship groups teetered in kitten heels along semi-sturdy soil divisions, desperate to either commune with nature or capture the perfect portrait against the flirtatious sea of colour.

We reluctantly left, giggling and waving as if the blooms were small humans.

Vivid floral memories frequently fill my thoughts when reflecting on my travels in Japan. A road trip through Kyushu's neighbouring Fukuoka, Oita and Saga prefectures one summer was equally flower-forward. From the comfort of the passenger seat, I was free to head-swivel, kilometre after kilometre, eye-spying countless ajisai (hydrangea) decorating the highways, cliff faces and gnarled back roads when we missed the turn-offs. Intensely coloured frothy globes sprouted from every rock crevice or verdant grassy slope we encountered: cornflower blue, snowy white, pale

Kochi Prefecture's famous Cosmos fields.

matcha green, musk lolly pink, grape and a deeper, regal murasaki (purple) – several tones I hadn't known existed until that moment, but which represented only a handful of the 100 varieties of hydrangea discoverable in Japan. I was in awe. I'd previously, and unfairly, considered this floral species 'old lady flowers'. On that trip, far from elderly, I fell in love.

I wondered whether flowers were something you learned to appreciate more with age and wisdom – as you become increasingly aware of your own mortality and the fleetingness of life. Or had I simply been blissfully unaware of their impact before?

Looking back, I now remember swooning over bright, buttery crops of spring nanohana (a type of flowering rapeseed or canola with mustard-flavoured greens) in the farming land of northern Kyoto's Ohara many years before. Equally, I conversed with proudly peacocking irises in shrine gardens from my 20s. In my 30s, I meditated over many a lotus and their sassy, water-lily sidekicks as they swam backstroke across reflective pond surfaces. On more than one giddy occasion, I'd been face-fondled by tentacles of wisteria or weeping willow. Once, as a teen, I licked a low-hanging plum blossom to embarrass my mum, who was trying to take a 'nice' photo. In my early 40s, a more grown-up appreciation allowed me to openly cry over an exquisite single camellia, the first to arrive on a temple shrub opposite my home, encased in the lightest frost like a sleeping beauty.

❀ A wonderful website for lovers of Japanese art, design and culture, Spoon and Tamago offer membership that includes access to their excellent 72 Seasons Newsletter (spoon-tamago.com). There are also several Japan microseason resources on creative platforms such as Substack or Patreon, and related podcasts. For the nitty-gritty, you should seek out translated Japanese texts.

The Floral Code

Flowers are represented extensively in Japanese art and design, traditional and modern, woven into all manner of textiles, etched or painted over pottery or lacquerware, and even hand-crafted into seasonal hair adornments worn by geisha to match their seasonally inspired kimono and obi (sash) ensemble. Flowers appear in family crests and decorative motifs, inspire architectural facades, structures and furniture detail, and are beautifully displayed everywhere from home tokonoma (vestibules for arts and culture) to grand hotel spaces and department store lobbies. Flowers act as offerings at public and private shrines everywhere from graveyards to makeshift neighbourhood versions.

Ikebana (Japanese flower arranging; also referred to as 'cha-bana' or 'tea flowers' when arranged for tea ceremony) (see p. 242) are a heightened form of decorative flowers, leaves, pods, reeds, grasses and the like, which pay homage to both passing and oncoming seasons, acknowledging nature's transience. The composition and preparation for each goes far beyond what the eye can see. The subtleties of the artform can take years of practice to even start to comprehend – but that's Japan all over. Ceremonial wagashi (most commonly soft namagashi) tea sweets (see p. 216) are themed by the seasons, frequently showcasing flowers. Japan curates some of the most stunning, fragrant flower shops on earth and embraces all species equally (even the much-maligned carnation and baby's breath), celebrating each in a way that is beyond inspiring.

On Reading Japanese Gardens

Knowing how to read a formal Japanese garden – at least the basics – will enrich your travel experience, whether you join a guided tour or wander at will. Appreciating gardens has been part of the Japanese culture for over 1000 years. Here I will share an overview of what I've gleaned by osmosis and from several Japanese garden aficionados.

Above: Be slow and mindful on Yatsuhashi (eight-plank zigzag bridges).
Below: Tomeishi says stop!

There's phenomenal choice in gardens throughout Japan – there are over 270 in Kyoto city alone. Most are regularly open to the public, some only on special occasions. The best are sublime, peaceful and inspiring.

Often referred to as Japan's 'great three' are Kanazawa's Kenroku-en, Okayama's Korakuen and Mito's Kairakuen. Each is magnificent, large-scale and historically significant, having been commissioned by feudal lords during the Edo period. However, there are so many incredible smaller, more intimate gardens to be wandered and absorbed, and these are frequently less crowded and easier to inhale.

Formal Japanese gardens often feature in the grounds of important cultural buildings such as the Imperial Palace or castle sites. They are commonly connected to temples, shrines, public parks and Botanic gardens. Those connected to Buddhist temples are often more structured than the freer-flowing strolling gardens of Shinto shrines, which lean towards a more natural look. Countless inner garden courtyards (tsubo-niwa) feature within high-end restaurants or shops situated in converted former homes or machiya (shop houses).

If you've seen photos or footage, you'll know Japanese gardens are not just about plants and the ways they are groomed or trained – these gardens often include many other design features such as bridges and stepping stones, stone lanterns or water basins, small waterfalls and streams, or ponds filled with koi, ducks and aquatic foliage. Gravel or sand is raked to mimic water bodies, plotted with rocks of wide-ranging shapes and sizes representing islands, mountains and sometimes objects like a ship, or an historic figure of note. Sometimes these rocks bear an inscription or poem. Barriers and trellises made from attractive natural materials such as bamboo, grasses, reeds or stones (like tomeishi, tied with natural fibre ropes and indicating 'no entry' – see p. 198), or the binding of certain trees to protect them from heavy snow or insects in different seasons, all add texture and information to individual settings.

Some feature 'borrowed scenery' (shakkei), blending in with the surrounding landscape; others tell a silent tale; some simply offer calm, balance and harmony. Here, the Buddhist concept of ma (empty space) adds a moment of pause to scenes, allowing better flow in the overall design. Various larger gardens can contain a mix of garden styles (dry, moss, wet and even secret nooks) that lay in wait for the curious. The Japanese have a way of subtly framing scenes to draw in your eyes and attention, enhancing your experience as you move from one angle to the next.

Asymmetry plays a large part in Japanese gardens, too; deliberately employed to promote a more natural look. Zigzag bridges (Yatsuhashi) or stepping stones across a pond or moss offer layered beauty in the form of mindfulness. Staying calm and focused ensures you'll note detail and arrive at your destination without ending up soaked and uncomfortable – another helpful life metaphor.

Stepping stones at Heian Jingu Shin-en, Kyoto.

Tips on Japanese gardens

▶ Perform a search in the area you plan to visit, and you'll be surprised how many spectacular little gardens are hidden around the country – some only open at certain times of the year. If something seems a bit remote or out of the way, start searching the map or the web for other features in the area that can add to your experience. Maybe that's temples, cafes, parks, museums, galleries, monuments or walks – whatever floats your boat.

▶ Despite my passion for Japanese gardens, I'm certainly no expert. I therefore gladly refer you to some talented folks who operate excellent guided (and sometimes self-guided) experiences: Kyoto Garden Tour (kyotogardentour.com), Kyoto Garden Experience (kyotogardenexperience. com) and Inside Japan Tours (insidejapantours.com) for delving further. Alternatively, enquire as to whether botanical gardens, garden societies, art galleries or other garden appreciation associations in your country run garden tours with local experts.

▶ Also acquaint yourself with Kyoto City Greenery Association and Oniwasan, whose excellent website documents over 1700 gardens (and counting) that have been visited by the website's owner–editor (kyoto-ga.jp).

▶ Perhaps you're drawn to bonsai or ikebana – both of which can be enjoyed throughout the year. Search for gardens, centres, exhibitions (held everywhere from museums, galleries and department stores to hotel lobbies and train station concourses), clubs or workshops. The seasonal blooming of bonsai is a sight to behold!

▶ Remember, most gardens look vastly different in each season. Some feature spring blossoms, while others are known for their autumn leaves or interpretative rock and sand scenes. There are also many 'four seasons' gardens that are wondrous year-round – dig deep to find out what resonates with you.

Above: Hakone Museum of Art's Shinsenkyo Garden, Kanagawa.
Below: Karesansui (dry landscape garden) at Enoura Observatory, Odawara.

Walking Meditations
– The Extraordinary Souvenir of Being Present

Exploring an attractive older section of a city at twilight feels otherworldly. Freshly rinsed stone paths, barely glowing paper lanterns and gracefully aged wooden structures surround me. I notice an obaachan (grandmother/elderly woman) in the distance. As I get closer, I admire her immaculately upswept hair and spotless, starched apron, neatly wrapped over a greyish cornflower-blue kimono. Her naturally hunched form is further bent over a flower pot, and she holds a small watering can. She nods, barely able to face my direction as I pass by. She sways slowly back and forth in an arc, spraying the ground around her building, purifying the entrance.

Above: Tiny neighbourhood Hokora (street shrine).
Below: Protective morishio (salt cone).

The pungent scent of dashi arrests my senses as I encounter an open kitchen window, which also emits the somewhat obtrusive fluorescent glow of overhead lighting. The gentle music of simmering pots competes with the sweet strains of a koto harp emanating from an upstairs room. I stop, listen and wonder at finding such comfort in something unfamiliar.

The sudden but polite ding of a bicycle bell alerts me that I'm standing in the way of a chef on a mission to deliver a remarkably stable stack of wooden trays filled with soba noodles. I realise that I've inadvertently wandered into a hanamachi (geisha district) – an epicentre of hospitality. Several of the covered doorways display a small plaque, a subtle form of traditional teahouse advertising that sometimes also declares the number of geiko and maiko that reside within. I almost trip over a knee-high rustic hand-pumped water station, which seems out of place and is clearly in the way. I assume it's obviously located for putting out spot fires in this timber-centric enclave. Later, I learn its purpose is to extrude soft water from an underground well connected to the pristine water system located in the surrounding mountains, ensuring easy water access for tea rituals.

Peeking through the window of what turns out to be a 400-year-old wagashi-ya (tea sweet specialist) – also conveniently located for the ceremonial tea 'set' – I'm drawn to a small dish of perfectly plated confectionery. Purposely off-set for the eye to follow are slender rods of kohakutou – translucent, crisp sugar-veiled sweets containing jelly firmly set with a single thread of yuzu zest. They mimic the zigzag bridges of a traditional stroll garden (see p. 187) – a Buddhist practice of mindfulness that forces one to slow down and 'be' in the moment. Entering a teahouse is a conscious act of letting go of the outside world and all it brings. It's an opportunity to revel in the quiet details – right down to the tiny sweets (see p. 236).

The skies grow darker. From the corner of my eye I catch the faintest flash of colour. Sensing movement, I turn to see two geisha scuttling in my direction, their gazes averted. I'm mesmerised. I now know not to approach or to ask for a photo – although I have in the past, when they were accompanied by an older geiko or okami-san (head of the okiya/house), who could provide or withhold permission. As they pass, I offer a polite bow which is acknowledged silently with a slight tilt of their heads. Their relief is palpable. I can't help but stare as they gracefully slip into a waiting taxi.

Only days later, on the opposite side of town, I find myself facing a nondescript yet strangely alluring entrance to a dark alleyway. It's barely the width of my shoulders, and the ceiling is just centimetres from my cranial vertex. I'd walked by previously without the slightest compulsion to enter, but today it practically jumps out and grabs me. I slip inside, moving towards daylight, past unmarked doors that lead to who-knows-where. I can make out one low-lit whisky den where a gold maneki-neko (beckoning cat) waves with metronomic timing from its tiny window box. I'm tempted – but instead, I exit into the fresh air of a tucked-away neighbourhood lane. I take a deep breath and scan my surroundings.

A solo flower is poignantly placed in a cracked concrete nook masquerading as a vase. The sun illuminates its petals. My emotions are mixed – it's beautiful, but is it in honour of a loved one lost? A few steps away, a ledge carved into a stone wall holds a small flask of sake, a fresh mandarin, still-burning incense, an offering to the deities. Beside it, a small stone statue wears a hand-knitted red bonnet and matching bib. My question is silently answered. Jizo statues (see p. 198) are not, as a client recently described them, 'dead babies'. Instead, they represent a popular deity responsible for guiding children who have crossed over (before or after birth) into the spiritual realm. I suddenly feel like an intruder, and my energy shifts. When I remember that O-Jizo-sama also acts as a safety totem for earthly travellers, I place a lucky five-yen coin at his feet, politely bowing in request of his service.

I release a long sigh, more audible than intended, and cast my eyes to the ground. Noticing my shoelace is undone, I stop to tie it and spot a tiny, perfectly formed cone of salt (morishio) sitting on a miniature dish beside a residential doorway, purifying the premise to eradicate unwanted negative energy or yurei (ghosts).

Stretching my arms to straighten my back as I stand, my gaze now lands on the tiled eaves of an old grocery store. A tiny pottery warrior perches there, staring down approaching enemies. Shoki-san, particular to Kyoto, is a handy fellow to have around, protecting homes and businesses from demons, fire, deception and injury. He faces away from the home, never looking directly onto another doorway lest he redirect the misfortune. I move along quickly, just in case, my clumsy foreign feet almost toppling a small red pail filled with water. It's another reminder that even the smallest ember is the enemy of a neighbourhood traditionally constructed of wood, as ineffectual as such a small water source might seem in the event of an actual fire. Perhaps, in another example of things unspoken (see p. 204), the quiet message of the pail works on a more subliminal level, reminding people to take care – and that can't be a bad thing.

Nearby, I spot a lost purse waiting for its owner on top of a ledge. I ponder how long it will take before someone drops it into the nearest koban (police box). I once saw an expensive pair of mittens placed on a manicured camellia bush in the hope the owner would return to retrieve them. They were still there weeks later, inside a clear plastic bag to shield them from inclement weather.

Generally, the Japanese are strongly law-abiding citizens, fearful of punishment and shame. The mittens remained on the camellia bush for the same reasons a vending machine filled with cans of alcohol can sit quietly on a residential strip without risk of being raided by underage drinkers, and why your phone, camera, laptop or handbag might still be found at the train station or park bench where you'd accidentally left it hours earlier.

I'm startled by the eerie horn-blowing of conch shells, signalling that Yamabushi (mountain monks) have descended from high in the ranges – special blessings available for a price assist with temple upkeep. Dressed in white robes adorned with colourful pompoms, they enter the laneway. A portly gentleman in an apron shuffles into sight from out of nowhere, requesting the blessing of his business – the Yamabushi follow in single file, down a dog-legged alleyway onto a broader path and into a small sake brewery. Hanging outside is a green sugitama (large cedar needle ball). It's a telltale sign that the new season's namazake (fresh sake) is underway – though it's not yet ready to drink, it will continue to mature until the ball turns brown. I listen to the Yamabushi's mystical incantations while I watch another lone monk much further down the strip wandering around a small and dusty empty block that's wedged between two low-rise modern apartment buidlings. He's performing a purification ritual before new construction begins.

I continue to walk for some time, my skin tingling partly from the growing cold, but also in recognition of the eclectic collection of small and mighty encounters I seem to be inviting. Finally, I turn the corner, ready to head for home. However, I stop in my tracks in disbelief as tiered pagodas, leafy ginkgo and low clouds create an extraordinary show of shadow puppetry against a mountainous backdrop. As the sun sets, my thoughts are lost in awe. Slowly and gently, I return

to conscious thought, honouring the silent stories that flourish in the unknown and reward curiosity.

As I grow more familiar and comfortable with my adopted home, I also become more daring.

On one occasion, I find myself with no plans for anything more than trailing my hands over book covers, gently fanning my face as I flick through the pages of the phenomenal selection of handsomely illustrated mooks on subjects from food, craft and design, travel, local happenings – all aimed at deciding which would come home for closer inspection. I adore Japanese bookstores (like Tsutaya, Maruzen Marunouchi and Kinokuniya) – even if they frequently have me searching for a bathroom, otherwise known as the Mariko Aoki phenomenon.

On this day, however, before I reach the bookstore I find myself sidestepping my usual route to trace the source of an intoxicating sweet and smoky vapour trail. It leads me to a small shop lined

Above: Maiko shuffling along Pontocho.
Below: Yamabushi blessings.

from floor to ceiling with small, coloured boxes – the keepers of neatly bundled stick, coil or conical incense – interspersed with essential accoutrements. Ethereal and grounding at once, traditional Japanese incense is very high quality, made from natural ingredients like tree bark, resin and spices, which are appropriate for the spiritual buildings and vestibules in which it is commonly burned. It's the antithesis of the cloying, mass-market varieties that remind me of the surfside bong shops of my youth, where we'd choke on sickly fumes crawling skyward out of lurid statuettes.

It's usually a temple or shrine visit that leads me to purchase incense (they make top-notch souvenirs and gifts – for yourself, if no-one else), but this time I find myself in a shopping arcade lined with bubble tea and novelty sock shops that leads through to a small, ancient temple encased within the modern structure. I take my time, leisurely padding around the intimate space, examining the wooden votifs (ema) neatly penned with prayers and wishes; strings of origami cranes, half of them faded from a back corner that lets in the sun; a vending machine filled with omikuji (fortunes) tightly rolled into miniature paper scrolls (some in English, which is still relatively rare) that are retrieved by a motorised dragon. I rub bronze statues for luck and bow to the Jizo solemnly tiered like a choir podium.

I relish having the space to myself in the otherwise busy arcade, and the fact there is no resident monk or omamori (amulet) vendor to warn me off when I wander into a shadowy side alley. With no indication that I shouldn't enter, no gate, rope or even tomeishi (see p. 187) to stop me, there seems no reason not to proceed.

I look around once again to ensure I'm not making a nuisance of myself, then boldly slip inside and quietly tiptoe all the way

Shoki-san and Ojizo-sama offer protection in different guises.

along the short but ice-cold tunnel, feeling extremely rebellious but strangely safe. Outside, I find myself surrounded by a tiny concrete oasis of mish-mashed pot plants and creeper-covered trellises, anchored by a pond with several large koi and an enormous duck. As I stand with my mouth open at the nonchalant inhabitants of this special little nook, it starts to snow. Delicate, fluttering flakes of ice crystals melt on my tongue, which has involuntarily poked out. I stand, frozen in the unlikeliness of the scenario, considering that there might be more moments like this.

In Japan, one story leads to another. It's like turning a corner from one street onto the next, where you suddenly find endless opportunities to learn more than you'd imagine possible about the country, its culture and yourself. You slowly re-engage with all your senses in a world where it's all too easy to switch to autopilot.

You know that trick where a

Just lit lanterns and twilight softly signal the transition to night and a heightened sense of mystery.

magician pulls seemingly infinite scarves out of a hat? Just when you think it's over, out hops a rabbit ... then more scarves, and finally a pigeon spreads its wings out of nowhere. Japan is a bit like that – the longer and closer you watch, the more you'll see – sometimes to the point of the ridiculous. Japan's abundance of visual information can be overwhelming for some, but by paring back the stimuli and focusing on smaller details, things emerge as informative, invigorating and thought-provoking.

Each walk raises my curiosity to discover more than what's at surface level – the what, why and how – along the way. Each new piece of information inevitably leads me down another track, heightening my awareness and understanding of my surroundings. These walks also bring me great joy and relaxation. Sometimes they help me process emotions that I've bottled up for too long. This is not uncommon in Japan, where travel can be surprisingly healing – try to be open to personal 'shifts' and the possibility of unexpected tears.

The meditative meanderings described above demonstrate how Japan looks, feels, smells and sounds to me when I'm actively participating in being present and wandering without agenda, but you won't find them in any guide – they have no route or addresses. They're merely a thread of memory snapshots from my happy wanderings and typical examples of what might be waiting for you. Your own walking meditation may look very different to mine. Try to let go of expectations – instead, be open to your walks being just as fruitful, and potential instigators for your own observations. Like many inclusions within these pages, my words aim to inspire more mindful travel and encourage you to take Japan at a slower pace – because it's the details that enrich personal stories.

Tips on walking meditations

▶ Before you start out on your own walking meditation, you might like to find a quiet spot like an empty temple deck, a leafy park bench, a patch of grass by a river or a tucked-away cafe and do some slow, deep breathing. When your head feels clear but energised, look around – what do you see, feel, hear and smell? Sit there gently noting until you feel yourself being drawn in a direction – then go for it. If you find yourself breaking out of the 'meditation', start again, or take a break to do something else completely. You can come back to your walk another day. There are no rules.

▶ If you come across an object you're unfamiliar with while wandering, perhaps take a picture and investigate it later online (think Google Images or Lens, or translation apps). The little bit of extra research may well inform you about a fascinating historic or cultural tidbit related to the very patch you walked, and this could direct you towards other places. Intrigue can grow rapidly, unfurling for as long as you allow it. While many Japanese

Look down. Tiny Fushimi-hokora neighbourhood shrines in a Kyoto back lane.

scenes are breathtaking and incredibly photogenic, sometimes it's the detail of an old letter box that can be truly stunning in an image when you take it as your focus, with the surroundings stripped away.

▶ If you love walking and have a good amount of travel time up your sleeve, perhaps consider a guided or self-guided walk over a few days or weeks. There are many trails around Japan that follow old postal village routes or temple pilgrimages. There are plenty of resources online, and companies like **Walk Japan** do an excellent job: walkjapan.com.

▶ If you're tired of walking, you can always hop on a train or bus to the outskirts of whatever city you're in – even if it's just a handful of stations away from the centre – and exit as you feel called to. Nothing is ever too far away to return from – and if you've recharged a little, it can be surprising how interesting a tiny, random neighbourhood can prove. Just remember to be respectful of residential privacy.

Cultural Faux Pas and the Eternal Unspoken

While I don't subscribe to tying yourself in knots over protocol (that's no fun for anyone), Japan does reward politeness and effort, so educating yourself on at least a smattering of Japanese pleasantries (greetings) and basic etiquette will likely prove more valuable than many other forms of 'travel' advice. Like adding grease to a door hinge, it doesn't require much time or effort, but it helps things operate more smoothly.

Blame it on the shoes

We were a little nervous as we approached the old ryokan, but thrilled that a complimentary meal in their restaurant was on the agenda. The local tourism office made us aware of that fact so that we didn't make other plans, but they'd asked us not to let on, so that our hosts could surprise us. No problem – my time in Japan had me well-versed in feigning mild shock and embarrassment, while also expressing gratitude and delight.

The owner popped out from behind the scenes to greet us and rattled off something in formal Japanese (keigo) that I didn't fully catch. I glanced at my husband for help, as he'd been working in the government school system and had a different set of language skills to mine. Ever helpful, he quickly whispered his translation.

'Our host has asked if we like to eat a lot of food.'

I quickly turned towards the proprietor and retorted, 'Mochiron!' – yes, of course! I patted my belly and showed off my best smile.

Our hosts looked at me silently, heads tilted like confused poodles. I then boldly added, 'We are Australian!' as if that would somehow explain it. We are clearly going to eat more – we are big, cheese-eating gaijin (foreigners).

After a prolonged awkward silence, our hosts' expressionless faces stuck in freeze mode, I was slowly scolded in a sombre tone. It turned out our translator was Korean, and so was generally more straight-speaking and unafraid to provide direct feedback. She advised me that my response was not appropriate given that the host had just generously offered us lunch in his restaurant. 'Yeah, of course, we're Australian' was not the best reply. I'm pretty sure everyone saw the colour drain from my face as I tried to explain away my faux pas, stressing that I was attempting humour and poking fun at myself.

Fortunately, they laughed, but from then on referred to me as Ms Mochiron (Ms Of Course). Luckily, mirth prevailed through the tension. At least, I think that's what happened. It's also possible they were simply relieved, or attempting to unburden me of my embarrassment and discomfort, which, in hindsight, might have impacted a potential review of their restaurant. It's not for me to know, but I accept what happened. It was my error, after all – not my first, and it certainly won't be my last.

Two decades later, departing from an incredible visit to a geisha house where I'd developed good relationships, one of my poor tour guests urgently ploughed through the genkan (entrance) – in just-replaced shoes – running across the tatami to vomit into the toilet bowl, almost ripping the shoji off in the process. Piercing squeals of 'Kutsu! Kutsu! Kutsu!' (SHOES!) from the young maiko (trainee geiko) hung in the air more acridly than the rapidly emerging aroma.

Walking impurities from outside into a home or business where people eat, sleep, work or entertain at floor level is considered abhorrent. Misunderstanding the hand gestures of a helpful co-traveller, who had tried to mime that the matcha they'd served had upset his stomach, the okami-san thought he was drunk! She remained composed, but her eyes were wild, her judgement ice cold.

I tried to explain and deeply apologise, while also trying not to make my guest feel even more uncomfortable. Later, I sent a formal letter of apology, followed up by a subsequent attempt to reiterate the apology. Even then, I never received a response, nor have they accepted a booking from me since. The owner may have been incensed or embarrassed, or maybe it was too difficult to express her feelings in English. Maybe it was convenient timing, with her maiko-san soon to debut as a fully fledged geiko (a role more financially beneficial than playing games while being quizzed

by curious foreigners). In the end, I had to let it go – which, by the way, is the appropriate action to heed if you repeatedly contact someone in Japan and do not receive a response. Take it as a sign that as one shoji closes, another opens – or just blame it on the shoes.

Even those of us who've spent significant time in Japan don't always get it right, and that's okay. Often when you're trying to impress just how much you know, you'll inadvertently announce yourself as a novice. Unless you are in a formal business situation, it's really about observing, informing yourself where possible, and giving it a go. Being able to laugh at yourself if you get it wrong – and you will – is crucial. Just be polite and genuine, especially with apologies, and don't try too hard.

There are rules for almost every situation in Japan, and it would take a lifetime of practice to learn and adhere to them all. If you fall down an etiquette research wormhole, you may well be too daunted to get on a plane. So don't do that.

Japanese footwear in fashion, art and culture.
Above: Modern Zori worn with Kimono.
Below: Enormous Geta sculptures at Daiyuzan-saijo-ji, Kanagawa.

Omotenashi – hospitality in the truest sense

You could tell from a distance that it was a cold and blustery morning down at Yobuku port, located on the far western tip of Karatsu in Kyushu's Saga Prefecture. Wildly bobbing fishing trawlers and tourist boats in cephalopod masquerade gave it away. The asa-ichi (morning market) was in full swing. With around a dozen stalls and a head count of under 50, it seemed the tiny adjacent fishing village was out in force, undeterred by a bit of weather, happily sheltered from the brunt of the icy sea breeze by a row of windswept shop houses.

With 90 per cent of the stalls selling whole fish or squid (ika) freshly plucked from just metres away, it was a struggle for my tour group to spend their money – which we dearly wanted to do because we couldn't see the marketeers selling out and preferred not to be viewed as unappreciative tourists simply gawking and taking photos. We sampled ika 'jerky', and ika-ten (a knobbly deep-fried version). We bought some teensy fish skeletons candied with sugar, soy and sesame, along with various other seafood senbei (rice crackers) to nibble at on the bus.

A ruggedly handsome fisherman caught my attention – his skin deeply tanned and sheened, like well-polished leather. His eyes twinkled and his gumboots were scratched up and muddied with fish guts and squid ink – who could resist? I approached his stall. Suddenly there were two of them, curious to know what had brought us there. They lifted a whole squid to my face so I could see how insanely fresh it was – shimmering skin, its body still writhing. A local woman trundled over in her wheelchair. She had mischief in her eyes and a clear hunger for banter – she was equally eager to know where we'd come from. Keen to further demonstrate the meaning of 'fresh', one of the fishermen pulled a knife from his

belt and deftly plucked two eyeballs from an unsuspecting carcass. He ate one and offered me the other. I politely declined, causing raucous laughter to ricochet throughout their posse and the neighbouring stalls.

A Taiwanese food tourist silently appeared and purchased a plate-sized fish, requesting that they slice into sashimi. She scoffed it on the spot. Now *there* was a woman who knew what she wanted – I admired her ingenuity. After posing for photos, I farewelled the fishermen and locals, sad that I'd likely never see any of them again. Nevertheless, I was happy to have made their acquaintance and a connection, despite the limitations of my Japanese and their non-existent English.

Further down the road, we abandoned our stroll to a beachside observation point when it started raining. Seeking warmth, we slid open the plastic weather-curtains of a remote roadside seafood shack, surprising the all-female group of volunteers who ran the remote

Just-caught squid at Yobuko Port, Karatsu.

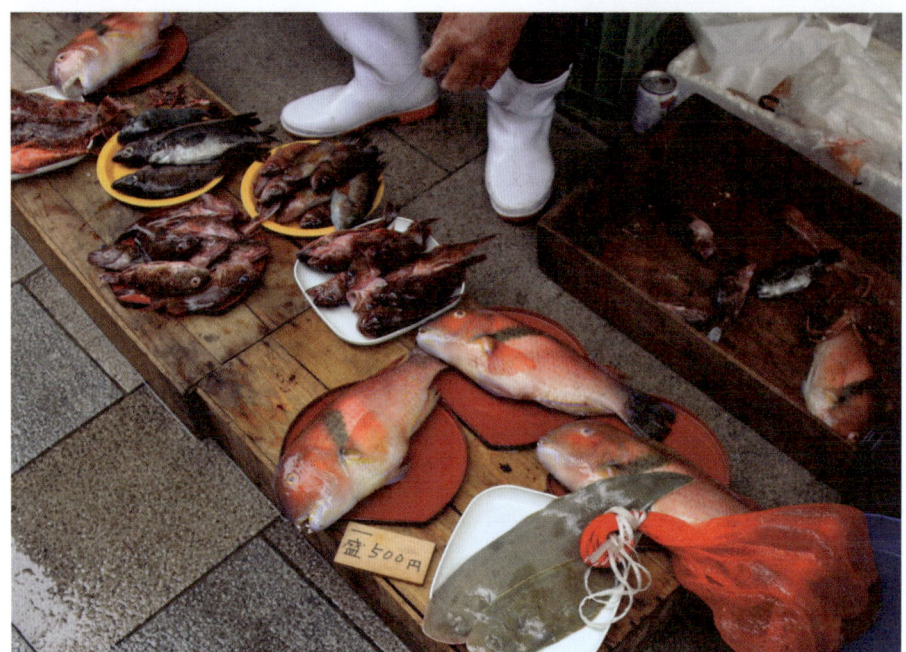

snackery purposed with keeping the village on the map. Bemused by our request to enter, they gestured towards rustic bench seats covered in plastic. We squeezed in, almost filling the space and ordered just a few bites – kaki (oysters), sazae (sea snails) and ika, grilled to order. We seasoned them with bench-condiments of soy, Kewpie mayonnaise, yuzu kosho (green chilli and yuzu skin paste) and shichimi (seven-spice mix). Again, the stallholders' fascination in us was as great as ours was in them. Once they warmed to our presence, they blushed like schoolgirls before happily posing for more photos. We were reluctant to leave, but lunch and vital ceramic shopping were on the agenda, Karatsu being just one of Saga's excellent pottery villages (see p. 152). The wares of well-known and commercial Arita and Imari villages (see p. 152) are easily detectable for their white porcelain bases, intricately painted with primary-coloured glazes. Karatsu-yaki, on the other hand, is based on a darker clay, with earthy grey and green glazes. These pieces are shaped more organically than their refined cousins. I appreciated both, but my small purchases from Karatsu are the ones that sing to me from my kitchen shelf when I make my morning coffee (see p. 252).

After a pleasantly salt-sprayed meander along a nearby beach, we'd worked up an appetite for lunch. My research had turned up what looked like a lovely restaurant in the middle of nowhere – I didn't know the region well enough at the time to have a regular favourite. Approaching a slightly run-down traditional building, I began to doubt my ability to spot a winner via educated guess – but entry provided a huge sense of relief. The space had been renovated into one large, open-plan room with an exquisite kitchen at one end – clearly the work of artisans, and possibly involving some reclaimed carpentry and cast iron irori (hearth) parts. The walls and floors were rendered smooth with polished concrete, and a large honeyed-timber table ran the width of the room. Typical of Japan, it was operated by a husband-and-wife team – him in the kitchen and her on the floor. As the only patrons, we were looked after like we were guests at a dinner party in their home. The food was simple but sublime – we ate local vegetables like yurine (lily bulb) dressed with sesame, and tempura of fuki no tou (bitter butterbur shoots), which flower earlier in Kyushu than other parts of Japan due to warmer weather. White fish sashimi, tucked into the folds of translucent daikon discs sliced so thin that they resembled rehydrated rice paper, were nabbed with fresh wasabi. Eel was stuffed with earthy burdock root and cloaked with a sweetened soy glaze. Slivers of pork and tofu were simmered in a delicate broth, then garnished with spring onion whites shredded as fine as dental-floss. Every mouthful revealed hints of an intriguing and sophisticated local food culture.

Just as delicious were the vessels in which they were served. As my companions drooled over them, our local guide enquired where our hosts had sourced the ceramics. Our hostess disappeared, but just as swiftly returned with the name and address of the artist's atelier, neatly handwritten on a perfect rectangle of textured washi. She handed it to my guide, who immediately informed us that it was nearby. Would we like to visit?

Up and up a nearby incline we forged, our poor driver struggling to prevent us from sliding downhill in the heavy rain, manoeuvring through tight streets better suited to foot traffic and bicycles. Perseverance won and we stepped out at the top of the hill into the finest mist. There, a family of monkeys lazily swung from trees to a corrugated iron shed-roof to vines. Here was a scene you're rarely far from in parts of regional Japan, but not often this close to town.

Our driver scurried to provide us with enough umbrellas to see us up a driveway too steep for the bus. The kind potter greeted us at the top and welcomed us inside, shuffling past his open workspace, where he'd clearly been busy creating until our interruption, and into a small but beautiful blonde wood gallery within his abode.

Through an enormous window, we enjoyed unadulterated district views as the hillside dropped away. We could see across the village below, right out to sea level. The potter kindly invited us to sit on the tatami before discreetly leaving the room, allowing us time to admire a few shelves lined with his work.

Before long, he and his assistant reappeared with trays of filled teacups and wagashi on individual plates with petite lacquered forks. Audible appreciation echoed in the intimate space before we all refocused on the view before us. A single plum tree nearby wore early buds like a pale pink spring brooch on a jumper of green. In this treasured moment, we were reminded of nature's collaboration with inherently occurring hospitality. Our host had no idea whether he'd make money from the group – his pieces were noteworthy and expensive. However, his priority was to make us feel welcome and comfortable, even though we'd hijacked his afternoon. There was no hard sell, no expectation – he was simply embracing the concept of 'ichi-go ichi-e' (loosely, that your first encounter is an unrepeatable opportunity to make a good impression), which sits comfortably with the practice of omotenashi – an innate form of hospitality that often pre-empts what the guest needs before they even realise it themselves. Needless to say, several pieces were snaffled.

Reflecting on the day, I could see that the hospitality of Karatsu had been with us all the way. What had been so unexpected and cool would never have happened without the interjection of our generous guide, who had attentively listened during our conversations and taken it upon herself to act and facilitate – without any expectation of commission or tip as a result. Born and raised in Fukuoka, our guide was justifiably proud of Kyushu and she wished to make our day as enjoyable as possible – it was her duty and her honour.

This was one of those travel days you remember for a lifetime – but in many ways, it was just another day in Japan. What's standard for the Japanese often feels so damn special for the rest of us.

Tips on Japanese hospitality

▶ While great hospitality is something you'll experience throughout the country, I have found that inhabitants of the smaller 'main islands' and those in more remote regions tend to go above and beyond. Their genuine sense of intrigue and desire to connect offers a natural form of hospitality. In many ways, this is luxury in its truest sense – even if it might not present that way at first.

▶ While the Japanese are on one hand excellent at pre-empting your needs when it comes to hospitality, they are also risk averse if something could appear to be overstepping. Be aware that sometimes, if you don't ask for something in a specific way, you may end up receiving less than you'd anticipated and closer to what you asked for verbatim. For example, you might request a restaurant booking for 7pm and be told there's nothing available. This is a response to your exact request. Instead, try rephrasing the question to ask what times (or nights) they have available for a reservation – that way, you may discover an availability at 6.30pm or

Ready for guests at Camellia Tea Ceremony, Kyoto.

7.30pm that night, or that the following night is wide open. Even recently I emailed back and forth for days with a chef requesting a range of dates for a booking. Each time they responded with an option for another date, before eventually revealing they were closing for two weeks ...

▶ Hotels, particularly ryokan, are an excellent way to experience Japan's top-notch hospitality (see my top picks on p. 265), most of them with an exciting food or drink element, and great service.

▶ Perhaps use a Japanese-to-English or English-to-Japanese translator on your phone if you have one. This can save time, confusion and embarrassment for both parties. Alternatively, you could try some creative hand signalling, which can end up being a lot of fun or a bonding experience.

▶ Feel free to excuse yourself (sumimasen/shitsurei shimasu) or apologise (gomenasai) more often in Japan than you might normally. It's deemed considerate.

Gut Instinct
– Eating Japan, a Multi-sensory Adventure

'Ii tenki ne?' ('Great weather, isn't it?') I asked the taxi driver en route to my lunch destination. Not original, but the harmless icebreaker was aimed at making him feel more comfortable with the gaijin who'd just invaded his inner sanctum.

Above: The Hassun – Kaiseki's scene-setting, seasonal declaration course.
Below: Pickled vegetables in Kyoto's Nishiki market.

The next three minutes were spent in friendly disagreement; him insisting my Nihongo (Japanese language) was pera-pera (fluent), while I vehemently but politely retorted that it was not. Exchanges like this are common between Japanese people and foreigners, whether the foreigner speaks three or 3000 Japanese words.

'Do you live here?' he asked.

'No, but I used to.'

'Ah, that explains it ... Are you on holidays? Working?' he continued.

'Eeto, muzukashii,' I told him – translating to 'Um, it's a bit difficult to explain.'

'I'm ... researching,' I went on.

'For your work? What do you do?'

I explained that I write about Japanese food and travel for various publications and that I also operate Japanese cuisine and culture tours. His eyes crinkled but shone in the rear-vision mirror, possibly considering how ridiculous he should find this concept.

'Ehhhhh!? Yumei desu ka?' (Whaaat? Are you famous?)

'I'm not.'

'Can you eat sushi?'

'Yes, of course—'

'Can you use chopsticks?'

'Yes, I can.' I smiled at him.

'What is your number one food in Japan?'

'Oh ... that is way too difficult to answer.'

'Come on, just one. Only one ...'

I tilted my head to the side for a long few moments before answering with something that I thought he might find interesting.

'Fresh handmade tofu or yuba (soy-milk skin).'

He looked a little shocked, but equally delighted. 'With shoyu?'

'Yes, with soy and freshly grated wasabi.'

He nodded approvingly.

'... but sometimes I like it with grated ginger.'

He almost jumped for joy.

'I also like yuba deep-fried into chips; they taste like pork.'

'Yes, yes.' He grew more excited by the minute. Then he tried to catch me out by asking, 'What about goma dofu?'

'Oh, I adore sesame tofu – particularly in winter when it's pan-fried so it's crisp on the outside and molten and custardy inside. But I also like it chilled in summer when it's like a cold savoury pudding.'

His slow, serious-faced nodding indicated approval. 'Soba! Do you eat soba?'

'Yes, in summer I enjoy buckwheat noodles with tsuyu (salty dipping broth); it's such a great stamina food. But in winter I love it with ankake (slightly sweetened, thickened dashi seasoned with soy), lots of negi (spring onion) and shoga oroshi (grated ginger).'

He started chuckling.

'What about natto?' he dared me. Natto are viscous (think okra-sticky), fermented soy beans with a funky, nutty, cheesy aroma and flavour, eaten with rice and commonly found unpleasant by Western palates.

'I don't mind it ... but the best I've had was one breakfast in Asakura (Fukuoka Prefecture)'.

'Nooo ... foreigners don't eat natto!'

'Sometimes they do. There's a place downtown that serves it over soba – frothy, with whipped raw egg and a good soy and dashi broth. It is divine.' I went on to explain where he could find it. He looked perplexed – how could this random foreigner possibly be informing him about something in his own city? Especially when it came to food – taxi drivers always know the best spots.

'What about fugu (poisonous puffer fish)? That's not good for you, right?'

'Actually, I find fugu a little boring flavour wise, although I was in Yamaguchi last week and enjoyed an excellent fugu kaiseki,' I said. I recalled the ten or so courses of fugu, including sashimi (wrapped around garlic chives with a squeeze of sudachi lime), nimono (simmered), karaage (fried) and nabe (hot pot).

'Ah yes, the region is famous for it, isn't it?

'Have you been to Yamaguchi, driver-san?'

'Not yet. You like tempura?' Clearly, he was the one who'd be asking the questions.

'Yes, particularly spring sansai (mountain vegetables).'

'What's your favourite yakitori?'

'I love tsukune with tare (sauce) and raw egg yolk, or simple sasami (breast) with shio (salt) and a little wasabi, or negima (thigh with spring onion), always with a side of crisp kawa (chicken skin) … and I was surprised to find chochin so delectable.' I recalled the surprising dish of unfertilised chicken egg yolk and oviduct, which hangs like the lantern for which it's named.

The driver cackled, shaking his head.

Only when he was satisfied did he begin to share his culinary intel with me, keen for me to know his top local joints – music to a food writer's ears.

*

For me, food forms the backbone of the best Japanese travels. One of the greatest pleasures in travelling the country is the discovery of old and new in every facet of the culture. Cuisine so beautifully demonstrates the coming together of a region, its people and their way of life. It seems that no occasion in Japan is without food reference or discussion. Whether you're on public transport, in a bar or cafe, or anywhere you meet people for the first or twentieth time, the conversation frequently leans towards food. Sure, it's a subject many of us make small talk over, but in Japan it's more of an obsession, and rightfully so.

It's possible to eat your way from one end of Japan to another and never lose interest. While you might see numerous washoku (traditional Japanese cuisine – recognised by UNESCO as an Intangible Cultural Heritage) dishes repeatedly served throughout Japan, it's also true that Japan's culinary diversity is colossal. Every pocket of the country boasts their own specialties based on climate and location-dependent agricultural history. Many restaurants specialise in a single category of cuisine – e.g. yakitori, tempura, sushi, ramen – and chefs commonly dedicate themselves to honing their craft until retirement.

Most Japanese people I've met are genuinely gleeful to be able to converse about their incredible cuisine with a stranger – their whole demeanour can change in that instant. Surprising people with my knowledge, passion and interest in culinary complexities has certainly earned me a level of trust and reward that I would not likely have received otherwise – and with that comes a ticket for peeling back another layer of Japanese experience. Here, I'm sharing just a taste of what's on the menu in Japan, information from which I hope you'll leapfrog – because, like most things in this country, the subject is deeply complex!

Eating Japan 101

RICE

An integral part of the Japanese diet (and culture), rice is served unadorned at most meals as a side but sometimes as a base for toppings. Donburi (rice bowl), for example, offers a splendiferous range of garnishes, from tempura (ten-don) and tonkatsu (katsu-don) to braised or simmered (nimono) dishes including Japanese curry or Kakuni (also known as Rafute: sweet soy pork) – all filling and affordable. My favourite is uber-comforting, sustaining and nourishing oyako-don (chicken, onions and barely cooked egg in a slightly sweet soy-seasoned broth). Gyu-don (topped with cheaper cuts of beef simmered in sweet soy broth) and una-don (grilled or steamed eel with sweet sauce brushed over it) are also popular. Variations on the rice theme include ochazuke (see p. 246), which is sometimes topped with grilled fish or vegetables before tea or dashi is poured over, and kaisen-don, where lush (predominantly raw) seafood blankets warm rice – imagine glossy salmon roe, fatty tuna sashimi, melting uni (sea urchin) and chunks of cooked crab meat (the best are found at markets and shops near fishing ports).

Zosui, ojiya and okayu are more often home-cooked but sometimes appear at hotel breakfasts, and are excellent when you're feeling a bit under the weather. These thin to thick congee-like rice soups are seasoned simply with one or more of the following: soy, nori, umeboshi, spring onions, sesame or fresh leafy herbs like shiso or seri (Japanese parsley).

Onigiri/omusubi (nori-wrapped rice balls) come with a variety of fillings – from a single pickled plum or slivers of tsukudani (kombu, mushrooms or other ingredients preserved in sweetened soy sauce) to modern tuna-mayo, avocado or fried prawns (such as Nagoya's specialty, ten-musu). These are great portable snacks and are available at specialty shops, depachika, supermarket, konbini (convenience stores) and occasionally from pop-up vendors.

Omurice (omelette cloaking seasoned or protein- and vegetable-studded rice, often topped with a rich sauce) in endless combinations is super filling. If you don't mind raw eggs, keep an eye out for tamago kake gohan (aka TKG) on menus – raw egg folded through hot rice with a specially designed soy-based sauce – total comfort at either end of the day.

YAKI-MONO AND AGE-MONO (GRILLED AND FRIED FOODS)

Yakitori-ya (yakitori eateries) pay homage to the simple pleasure of chicken on the grill. This is one of my top picks for a casual evening meal with friends. Yakitori isn't hard to find in Japan, but some cheaper ones, situated near universities or under railway tracks, taste of kerosene smoke and are best left for end-of-night booze romps when you can't tell the difference. Ideally, only order a couple of items at a time, allowing the chef to continue cooking and serving other customers before returning for your next selection. Other grilled stick (kushi) food commonly including beef, pork and vegetables is called 'kushi-yaki', while crumbed, deep-fried stick food is kushi-katsu – collectively they are kushi-mono (stick foods).

Note that chicken restaurants specialising in local chicken (jidori) typically offer multi-course meals involving a variety of chicken parts and organs, and preparation methods (sashimi, grilled, simmered and more), and often include eggs in some form, perhaps an omelette, TKG or purin ('pudding', think crème caramel or thick-set custard). Such establishments can be expensive, but they are the only places I recommend eating chicken sashimi – never at a cheap izakaya or similar. I've not been sick from raw chicken in Japan, but I am very fussy about how and where I eat it – the chicken must be super fresh, the chef knowing exactly where, when and how it was raised and dispatched. I have, however, been ill from river-fish sashimi – though this may have been from not adding an adequate amount of apparently bacteria-retarding fresh wasabi! Yep, be sure to always eat it, particularly with river-fish, which are more prone to carrying parasites that would normally be killed during the cooking process.

Literally meaning grilled meat, Yakiniku typically includes beef (gyu-niku), pork (buta-niku), vegetables (yasai) and sometimes seafood (umi no sachi – blessings of the sea), grilled over charcoal, usually DIY style. At teppan-yaki (more expensive, high-end counter restaurants) your meal is expertly cooked for you over a hotplate or teppan. In seaside areas it's popular to BBQ your own food. Think winter oyster shacks, or fresh Kochi bonito over straw flame. In Mie, let Ama (pearl/abalone free divers) do the honours.

✽ **Wagyu** (high-quality, carefully raised and finely marbled Japanese beef) can be incredible, but, again, don't be taken in by promotion. While the origins lay with the Tajima cow breed (first introduced to the Kobe region), beautiful Wagyu is now bred in various parts of Japan – each of them offering the essence of regional terroir. Older dairy cattle, many from Hokkaido, are also being better utilised these days, and it can be delicious in proficient hands. If you just want to see what the fuss is about, sampling a few Wagyu slivers at an upmarket izakaya, where splitting dishes between a group is standard, further reduces the cost. Relatively small amounts of the rich, delectable beef can be highly satisfying.

Agemono – fried foods – are popular in Japan and eaten regularly in small quantities combined with a variety of other healthier foods. However, it becomes the star of the show at exceptional tempura (fried seafood and vegetables) and tonkatsu (quality pork, crumbed and fried) counters. I'm always up for fragile tempura served with Japanese sea salt (Kyoto style) or ten-tsuyu dipping sauce, or perfectly tender tonkatsu – with its special thick 'Worcestershire-inspired' sauce and toasted sesame, sides of rice, raw shaved cabbage (which helps digest oily foods), soup and pickles. Jumbo fried prawn (ebikatsu) or croquette (korokke) are popular sides or alternatives.

My pick is rich rosu (sirloin) or a mix of it and hire (tenderloin or fillet). Sometimes I take it topped with curry sauce (katsukarē) – my husband and brother are huge fans of the very reasonably priced curry chain CoCo Ichibanya, where there are also plenty of plant-based options.

NIMONO, MUSHIMONO AND AEMONO (SIMMERED, STEAMED AND DRESSED) FOODS

Nabemono (hot-pot foods) – named for the donabe (ceramic or cast-iron vessel) they are simmered in – are highly popular in winter, when they are often cooked tabletop over a portable burner and served family-style from the central vessel. Many restaurants include nabe on the menu during the season, packing them with delicious fatty fish varieties and other sublime seafood like crab and oysters, or game meats like wild boar (inoshishi – the main ingredient of botan (peony) nabe), duck (kamo nabe) and deer/venison (shika) meat – alongside winter veggies

Sukiyaki in Matsusaka and oyster BBQ in Ise, Mie Prefecture.

like daikon and their greens, turnip (kabu), cabbage (hakusai), leafy greens (like komatsuna or mizuna) or other root vegetables like burdock (gobo), lotus (renkon) or taro. This is a great way to increase your vegetable intake – which I emphasise because I often hear people complaining about the lack of vegetables when dining in Japan. However, it's actually about knowing where to find them.

Shabu-shabu (onomatopoeia for the sound ingredients make as they are being swept through simmering broth with chopsticks to cook them) and sukiyaki (thinly sliced beef and onions simmered in sweetened soy, dipped in raw egg if desired) are popular forms of nabe found all over Japan.

Nikujaga (beef and potatoes), Chikuzen-ni (chicken and root vegetables) and Furofuki daikon (bathing daikon) are further popular examples of simmered dishes, as is Curry (kare) – which, perhaps surprisingly, deserves its own category. They are often served with some form of protein, e.g. 'katsu' or vegetables, over rice or noodles. Hokkaido's delicious, brothy soup curry is commonly packed with chicken pieces and locally grown vegetables like pumpkin, corn and potato. I'm a sucker for a kare-pan (curry-filled fried bread; basically a savoury doughnut).

Steamed foods (mushimono) are healthful ways to serve meats, seafood and vegetables, capturing their vitality. They are often served or dressed with soy or vinegar-based sauces (aemono). Chawan mushi – steamed savoury 'custard' – is one of the best examples of steam cuisine in Japan, much loved for its elegant simplicity. Dressed vegetable (and other) side dishes typically highlight a few favoured dressings, e.g. goma-ae (sesame) or shira-ae (tofu), while vinegared dishes are known as sunomono – mozuku-su being one palate-refreshing example of seaweed in vinegar.

Casual eating and drinking

IZAKAYA

This is my favourite way to eat – share plates of deliciousness with sake. The staggered ordering style encouraged at yakitori-ya also applies at quality izakaya, literally 'sake shop'. Formerly, sake was the focus but in modern times food became an essential player. A good izakaya should serve excellent sake (nihonshu) alongside its selection of small plates for sharing. Beer and shochu based cocktails are also popular at izakaya these days, including fresh fruit chuhai (shochu, freshly squeezed citrus juice and soda), or a range of other flavours including Calpis (a sweet, fermented yoghurt drink – one of my guilty pleasures; I also love seeing people's reactions when they think I'm ordering cow piss).

Better izakaya tend towards more succinct menus, often only available in Japanese and displayed on the wall – whereas cheaper, occasionally rowdier options cater to university students or families on tighter budgets. As a general rule, the better the food and drink, the more expensive, but even a great izakaya won't break the bank.

You'll find clusters of very local izakaya conveniently located near train stations – zoom in to your station of choice on an online map and type in 'izakaya' to instantly locate the larger huddles, excellent for izakaya-hopping. Also look for shotengai (arcades with old-fashioned shops and eateries) and yokocho (side streets and alleys often lined with izakaya, bars and small food-related shops).

'B' or 'B-kyu gourmet' is a general term coined to honour quality, fuss-free eateries – think deliciously comforting and nostalgic rather than slick and polished, minus the 'gourmet' price tag. Dishes in this category may include: hayashi rice (topped with hashed beef and demiglace sauce), curry rice or noodles, hambaagu (minced/ground beef patty topped with a variety of sauces or an

Lunch Specials

Popular at lunchtime are teishoku (set meals), commonly served on a tray, based on the Japanese 'everyday' meal structure of ichiju-sansai (literally one soup, three dishes), composed of soup (shiromono or suimono, usually miso), a protein (e.g. grilled fish (yaki-zakana) or fried chicken (karaage)) and two side dishes (usually vegetable-based, often simmered (nimono) and dressed (aemono)), sometimes steamed (mushi-mono), always served with rice (gohan) and pickles (tsukemono). Ideally, it embodies Washoku's (traditional cuisine) fivefold principles: five colours, five tastes, five cookery methods, five senses, and appropriateness (tapping into nature and community – location, occasion, heart, etc.).

A great way to keep up your nutrient intake when travelling (as it includes legumes, seaweed, tofu and more), teishoku is found in local eateries throughout the country, from family restaurants and shokudo (canteen) eateries popular with office workers to more upmarket venues. Bento (compartmental food boxes) offer a compact, portable version of similar foods – perfect for train travel and picnics. Train stations (eki) offer regional-specialty bento known as eki-ben.

Hot tip – lunch at cream-of-the-crop establishments is often more affordable than evening dining – even if it's for the same menu.

Above: Teishoku lunch in Kochi's eggplant and ginger fields.
Below: Rice soup (ojiya/zosui) with pickles.

egg), yakisoba (stir-fried noodles with meat, cabbage and ginger pickles), motsunabe (innards stew) and monjayaki (Tokyo-style 'flat' okonomiyaki).

Homestyle dishes (like Kyoto's healthful, interesting obanzai) differ from region to region and are worth seeking out at charming, usually 'mom-and-pop' run eateries.

Kissaten are nostalgic, old-school cafes serving pour-over coffee and light snacks. The mid-morning BLT with Japanese mayo and mustard on offer at many kissaten is a rite of passage. Some still allow smoking (see p. 268). There are also gazillions of contemporary cafes with relaxing, atmospheric or sophisticated Zen interiors. Coffee joints are 10,000 times better than those from 15 or 20 years ago – now, local roasteries offer coffee-tasting flights, some accompanied by matching foods.

Breakfasts

Traditional Japanese breakfasts – typically grilled (dried or fresh) fish, vegetables, rice, egg, pickles and tea – are usually taken at home. However, stay at a ryokan or modern hotel with a Japanese restaurant attached and you'll likely be in luck (but allow time in a high-end ryokan as breakfasts can be quite formal, following in the kaiseki style). Independent restaurants serving Japanese breakfast in larger cities are few and far between, and Western restaurants serving egg dishes are still slim pickings, or simply open too late (if you have an early start, pre-purchase and refrigerate a yoghurt or tamago-sando (egg sandwich) for morning. Alternatively, convenience stores are your best bet, or waiting until 11.30, when lunch service starts. Some early-opening cafes and bakeries offer 'morning service' (a boiled egg, toast and coffee, or similar).

LOCAL DELICACIES

There will be foods, including some already mentioned, that may challenge your brain, palate and/or ethics. Please try to remember you are a visitor observing another culture.

Unaware that foreigners might find it offensive, a fishmonger once proudly showed me his display of whale meat, blubber and 'bacon', enquiring as to whether we ate whale in my country. When I told him we didn't, he seemed to pity me. It would be a shame if everything we believed 'wrong' about a destination's choice or culture was whisked from our sight (which I've seen happen in Japan's best-known fish markets) – how would we learn about other places and ourselves? The consumption of whale has a complex history, but it's not my story to tell. Differences are part of the joy of travel. Exercising patience and reserving judgement are crucial. If you find that you cannot, at least be prepared to avert your eyes if you see bear or seal curry in a can, or live seafood dispatched in front of you at dinner, an act that demonstrates freshness. Try not to stumble into a horsemeat or tongue specialty restaurant if such things make you uneasy. Flame-grilled whole sparrows – beaks, skulls, guts, claws and all – were a challenge even for me.

FAST FOOD AND QUICK BITES

Although I try to avoid fast foods, they are highly popular for reasons of affordability. Japan boasts a range of both local and international chains, which are often better quality than at home. MOS Burger's teriyaki chicken wedged between compacted grilled rice 'buns' or Freshness Burger's juicy patties with pert salad ingredients are my pick, for convenience.

On that topic, I'm a bit tired of hearing how fabulous Japan's convenience store (konbini/conbini) foods are when there are so

many decent, affordable alternatives. While they might have a phenomenal selection of better and cheaper options than in my own country, they are still predominantly a convenience store – in every sense of the word. They're great for luggage forwarding, or when in need of a toilet, and if you're local, for paying bills and buying event tickets. For me, konbini are perfect for in-room picnics at the end of a long day when you can't walk another step, or when you're on the hop between places and in critical need of a snack – and yes, the constantly changing and seasonal ice-cream game is off the charts, as are the chips (crisps).

Sure, mass-produced konbini tamago-sando (egg sandwiches) are cheap and tasty enough – but you'll find better at a pan-ya (bakery), especially those with good oyatsu-pan (snack breads with an incredible variety of savoury and sweet fillings or toppings) or a depachika (food hall under a department store). And, I'll admit, it's fun to watch an onigiri wrap itself in nori (if you follow

Hand-crafted soba and sweets in Seto city, Aichi Prefecture.

the instructions). I've even succumbed on occasion to Famichiki (boneless fried chicken), although I prefer nikuman (meat-filled steamed buns – usually pork or beef) – but to eat at a konbini can rob you of the experience of dining somewhere with inexpensive, delicious and often healthier food and wonderful local hospitality and culture.

An occasional food for many due to high salt and fat content but highly popular with workers or students on the hop, ramen (alkaline wheat noodles) are so 'fast' they're sometimes slurped while standing. If time is not of the essence, a side of juicy gyoza or fried rice is the go. Soup for ramen comes as varied as the region and creativity allows, and the same/similar noodles are also used in yakisoba. Healthier menya (noodle) options like soba (buckwheat), udon and somen (wheat) are seasonally served hot or chilled with dipping sauce or in broth. Other drink or snack (including sushi) 'standing bars' are designed for grab, guzzle and leave scenarios.

It is considered rude to eat while walking, so street food is not as popular in Japan as other parts of the world, with a few exceptions: festival foods (think okonomiyaki and don't hate me for preferring Hiroshima-style, please!), dorayaki (including the fish-shaped taiyaki) (see p. 236), stick food, takoyaki, kakigori and onigiri. Recently, heavily touristed areas are allowing nibbling while strolling to keep the crowds moving. Yatai (street carts, usually with seating) commonly serve ramen, gyoza, yakitori, oden or izakaya-style dishes, and these are famously found in Fukuoka city, but small huddles can be found elsewhere, including Osaka, Naha (Okinawa), Kochi (Shikoku) and Obihiro (Hokkaido). Options for grabbing other quick and easy takeaway meals are exhaustive – from bento boxes to depachika salad bars, you'll be spoilt for choice.

Formal dining

Traditional **Kaiseki-ryori**, carefully choreographed multicourse dining (sometimes referred to as Japan's haute cuisine), developed from humble roots in Buddhist tea ceremony. Widely believed to have inspired a lighter shift in Nouvelle Cuisine from the 60s onwards, Kaiseki typically features around 12 intricate and exquisitely presented courses of highly seasonal, specialty ingredients, cooked in a defined order and served on rare and beautiful tableware. Kaiseki is predominantly enjoyed at elegant restaurants known as ryotei or in ryokan (Japanese inns with breakfast and dinner usually part of the package).

Tip – Doing an outstanding job of making this culinary artform more accessible for travellers, Hoshino Resorts' Hoshinoya and Kai properties offer in-house kaiseki, highlighting the food craft of each region.

Slightly less formal is **Kappo-ryori** (chef-centric counter style cuisine), which often leans more creative, flexible and interactive in approach – served omakase (chef's choice) style. A top-notch Sushi-ya (sushi-restaurant) or Tempura-ya are good examples of Kappo-style dining. I adore the mindfulness of service at a first-rate tempura counter, where items of pristine seafood and vegetables are delicately deep-fried and served to order, one stunning morsel at a time. It's a far cry from the 'basket' of tempura moriawase (assortment) you've tried at your neighbourhood Japanese joint back home.

In Japan, internationally influenced fine dining and higher-end creative dining is second-to-none. The number of awarded Michelin stars, should you buy into that kind of thing, is phenomenal given the size of the country. You'll find a stack of information online, but I've included several personal recommendations below.

WORTH THE SPLURGE

Hokkaido

· Le Musée (Sapporo), Ryotei FUMOTO, Sushidokoro Kihara (Hakodate), Takazawa (Niseko).

Kanto

· **Tokyo** – Abysse, Censu, Craftale, Crony, Den, Florilège, jinen, Julia, Lature, L'eau, L'Effervesence, Nippon Cuisine (Hoshinoya Tokyo), Noda, Ode, Sio, Shirosaka, Sushi Wasabi, Tempura Motoyoshi, Yakitori Hinata, Wineshop & Diner FUJIMARU.

Chubu

· **Ishikawa** – Fuwari, Hosho Sushi, Installation Table Enso (Kanazawa), Mimasu Sushi (Kahoku), Flatt's (Noto).
· **Aichi** - a.ligne, le Lotus (Nagoya).

Kansai

· **Kyoto** – Ajiro Honten, Badu, Bini, Cenci, Chef's Table by Katsuhito Inoue, Coppie, Fudo, Fujii, Gyuho, Koke, Kosa, Kyoto Wakuden, La Bûche (Ohara), LURRA, Moko, Monk, MOTOÏ, muroi, Orto, Ryozen, Tan, Tempura Matsu, Tempura Ten-you, Tozentei, Ueru, Wabiya Korekido.
· **Shiga** – Kyogoku Sushi, Uosen (Shigaraki).
· **Hyogo** -Kyoto Cuisine Takagi, Cuisine Inn Takasago.

Shikoku

· **Kochi** – Aizen, Auberge Tosayama, Jiro No Ouchi (Hatayama), La Prima Vorta.

Kyushu and Okinawa

· **Fukuoka** – Roojiura no Shiki, Shinmiura Hakata Honten,

GohGan, Wine and Sweets Tsumons.
- **Saga** – Arutokoro (Karatsu).
- **Okinawa** – Mahae, Robata Shirakachi.

Dining this way is a treat worth saving up for. However, you don't need to seek out the best known and often most expensive establishments. I've been disappointed by several famous kaiseki restaurants – yet another reminder not to get hung up on hype, or other people's opinions. The cuisine of more humble, accomplished chefs or quiet up-and-comers can be far more impressive – I know some brazen, boundary-pushing characters among them who produce truly inventive cuisine – so it's worth trying your luck in places with more affordable menus before they are recognised and can therefore raise their prices.

Incidentally, ordering sushi or sashimi moriawase in a good izakaya, or casual sushi joint, or locating a reputable kaiten-zushi (conveyor belt sushi) is a splendid (less intimidating) way to sample both before you spend top dollar on a high-end experience.

Sweets

It may be hard to believe, based on the proliferation of Japan's spectacular patisserie, bakeries, cake, dessert and chocolate shops, but certain sweet foods were unknown until relatively recently. Serving dessert after a meal was uncommon unless it was fruit. In fact, affording foods containing sugar (including Kyoto's sweet, creamy saikyo miso, sometimes used in traditional confectionery) was a sign of wealth at various stages in history where sugar, like salt and rice, acted as currency.

Setting aside the stunning ceremonial and ornate seasonal wagashi, equally popular and enjoyed casually with tea are various simple sweets like dango (glutinous rice dumplings with sweet toppings, like mitarashi-dango with black sugar and soy glaze), mochi (including daifuku-mochi – glutinous rice 'dough' wrapped around sweet bean paste, some containing fruit like strawberries), manju (a baked, steamed or griddled flour-based dough containing bean or other pastes), dorayaki (gong-shaped treats made from sandwiching bean paste, custard or flavoured creams between two small pancakes) and monaka (wafer casings filled with similar, and more recently served as dessert filled with ice cream). Most of these sweet morsels can be found served in tea salons and specialty shops, at depachika and around temples or shrines, where you can sometimes watch them being made.

Summery kakigori (shaved ice with sweet syrup poured over) is probably the closest thing to what we might think of as dessert, and it's thousands of years old. It has recently experienced a resurgence in popularity, modernised to include a belly of hand-crafted ice cream, or slathered with fresh fruit compotes, nutty foams or fragrant cremes, in flavours such as azuki (red bean), ginger, yuzu, matcha, shiso, pistachio, chocolate, coffee and vanilla. Sometimes, flower waters or alcohol are added. And that's just the tip of the iceberg, if you'll forgive the pun.

You can't taste the sweet without knowing the bitter

The full details of my first tea ceremony are but a scant memory, despite its lingering impression. At around the age of 18, I was holidaying with my mum and aunt, staying at a ryokan for the first time. We were ushered in with what felt like an enormous amount of formality, and I remember feeling harried. They bundled us into our room, where we were ordered to the floor before the door rather abruptly shut. We were suddenly captive. Fearful about what would happen next, we stayed glued to the tatami. Soon after, the door slid open and, to our relief and delight, we were served welcoming sencha (quality green leaf tea) and sweet senbei wafers inked with pretty flowers before our server disappeared again. Finally starting to relax, we bravely stood up, ready to make a move, yet too worried to leave because we weren't sure when and where to remove our shoes without making a scene. We amused ourselves by wandering in circles around the sparsely decorated room, sliding open cupboard doors to find the futon (mattress), soba (buckwheat kernel) pillows and little else, all the while thinking 'What the heck do we do now?'

I recall scowling from the window of our first-floor room, dismayed by the tangle of electrical wires hanging between telegraph poles, obstructing the view of shophouses across the lane. These were the same wires I grew to adore as an integral part of the Kyoto landscape. When the sun sets behind the forest of power links, especially at the end of a long major boulevard, their dramatic black silhouettes appear to cradle the violet and pink of the moody twilight, seemingly slashed wide open by a katana (sword) – a scene so oddly natsukashii (nostalgic).

A sharp and sudden rap on the door announced the entrance of our okami (mistress of the house), catching us completely off guard. In my haste to return from the bathroom, I left the toilet slippers on and launched back onto the tatami – rookie error. Okami-san silently scolded me – her eyes telling me all I needed to know – and the situation was swiftly rectified.

We became so concerned with doing the wrong thing that when she left again we sat, barely breathing, around a squat lacquered table. I nervously cracked open a bottle of goldleaf-flecked sake, a keepsake from Takayama intended for home – this was an

Foodie highlights and shopping

▶ Booking accommodation with a kitchenette allows you to play with the fresh ingredients you can't take home. Look for refurbished machiya (former merchant shophouses) mostly found in Kyoto and Kanazawa (try Kyoto Machiya Stay, Machiya Residence Inn, Machiya Inns & Hotels or Iori Machiya Stay), an Airbnb, ski lodge or apartment hotel – like those from the excellent Mimaru Hotel Group. Fairfield Inn by Marriott hotels contain a communal space kitted out with heating facilities, conveniently adjacent to Michi-no-Eki (see below), where visitors are encouraged to eat or shop for local foods. Check out farmstays, too.

▶ Michi-no-Eki – These road stations found all around Japan are for dining, shopping and restrooms. Meals and souvenirs often feature locally grown or made foods and crafts (particularly in regional areas), providing a peek into the community and its cuisine. In remote alpine areas, you will sometimes find special mountain vegetables, medicinal herbs and sometimes insects – the latter two occasionally steeped in sake or shochu as remedies. Also be on the lookout for farmers' markets.

▶ Depachika (under-department-store food halls) offer one or more floors of fresh, high-quality produce and premade foods of all kinds (Japanese microwaves have 'crisp' settings for fried foods) – all perfect for picnics or eating at your accommodation. Some items like tea, soy

and soy preserves (tsukudani), pickles (tsukemono) or beautifully boxed rice crackers (senbei) make excellent foodie souvenirs for home. Miso also makes a great gift, in all its regional styles, but don't carry in your hand-luggage, as it's considered a liquid.

▶ Brilliant food markets, gourmet stores and high-end supermarkets are often found in and around main train station buildings or in upmarket neighbourhoods. These sites are gold for local culinary souvenirs, or omiyage (the Japanese practice of bringing a local food gift or similar when returning from a trip).

▶ Shotengai are oldschool arcades or strips lined with shops, including a good selection of fresh and less perishable foods, found in cities and regions throughout the country – perfect venues for witnessing locals going about their daily lives.

▶ Some large cities boast antenna or satellite stores stocked with premium food and craft from a particular prefecture. For example, in Tokyo you'll find Nagano, Fukushima, Okinawa, Yamagata and beyond in Nihonbashi (the former location of Tokyo's first marketplace) and Ginza. Some stores specialise in the best regional foodstuffs and utensils from all corners of Japan – for example, Akihabara's Chabara and Akomeya (various locations).

▶ Japan offers a smorgasbord of activities and experiences for serious cooks and foodies, including a broad range of cooking classes, food-and-drink-related day tours, tastings, specialised workshops for products like sake or miso making, fishing, farming and seasonal harvesting. As a quick guide: spring offers rice planting, tea picking and bamboo shoot digging; summer offers orchard fruit picking; autumn is the rice harvest along with grapes, apples and mushrooms; and winter offers citrus and strawberries. Seaweed is harvested year-round, but the majority happens between winter and spring.

▶ Source great local tea, tea sweets and locally crafted tea vessels or implements (such as cast iron kettles, ceramic teacups, bamboo whisks and tea scoops) in tea-growing hubs, specialty tea or accoutrement shops or department stores, or in Geisha/teahouse precincts.

emergency. Soon after came another short knock and the shoji (translucent paper and timber-latticed room partition) immediately slid open. We sat bolt upright, ready to be schooled on our next error in judgement, when our host changed tack by inviting us to a tea ceremony in the garden.

Unsure what to expect but certain that we should not refuse, we followed her, wearing the correct slippers this time, transferring to geta (wooden flip-flops) at the edge of the garden. We tottered over neat stepping stones to a larger stone in front of the ochaya (teahouse) where we were instructed to remove our footwear, and then, without letting our feet touch the ground, crawl through a small square cut from the teahouse wall. This traditional way to enter ensures all tea recipients are humbled – literally on the same level, disregarding status (in a country where hierarchy is heeded) before the ceremony commences.

Even in my teens, and much trimmer than my current form, entry proved something of a challenge. My petite mother was okay, but my dear aunt's fulsome hips made for an extruded and comedic arrival, at least for the three of us. Barely containing ourselves, we collectively reached the point of tears. Desperately attempting a serious facade only worked us up further. Fortuitously, being jammed inside the tiny teahouse with no room to unravel temporarily tamed our yearning to roll around on the ground crying with laughter. Like embarrassed children scared of upsetting our sensei (teacher), we continued to feign attentiveness as the walls closed in on us. Suddenly, the tension burst like an overblown balloon, deeply irking our already unimpressed host. Okami-san was pissed.

My first ryokan experience and tea ceremony (chanoyu, chado or sado – the Way of Tea) certainly didn't exude the kind of hospitality Japan is known for. However, I'd like to think that way back then, when so few foreigners were travelling to Japan, our

hosts simply didn't know what to do with us. Similarly, we had little way of knowing what to expect or how to react, given the insufficiency of reliable translations at the time.

It's a wonder I went back for more, but I've enjoyed countless chanoyu since and no two have been the same. I now believe that attending a tea ceremony as one of your first cultural encounters in Japan can offer grounding and help travellers to appreciate the subtlety that exists throughout the greater culture. Tea ceremony also connects you with a local or several and, when done right, issues the ultimate welcome. Spend more time in Japan and you may find out that experiencing the ritual in the home of a friend who's been practising since childhood is a sublime treat and an incredible privilege.

Non-verbal communication (see p. 268) is such an interesting part of travelling Japan, but rarely is it as integral to the enjoyment of the experience as it is during tea ceremony. Imagine yourself seated silently on the tatami of a chasitsu (traditional tearoom within the ochaya) – an intimate timber construction with earthen or paper-covered walls. While you're waiting for the ritual to begin, you note the gentle scrape of the sliding partition announcing the host/pavilion master/practitioner's arrival, and then the soft swishing of a kimono hem or tabi (split-toe socks) as your host settles into place. Already on their knees, they bow deeply, slowly scooting into position by the tea paraphernalia.

Focus, and you'll hear gently bubbling water announcing its readiness for purifying crucial implements for the making of tea. Note the quiet and careful selection of the bamboo ladle; the dip and trickle of water as it cleanses the tea bowl and utensils; the barely audible sound of fukusa (ceremonial silk cloth) that dries all and is then folded away with origami precision. Listen for the hushed swooshing of the chasen (bamboo tea whisk) as it whips around the matcha (powdered superior-quality green tea). Is that gentle birdcall from the garden's water bowl outside? Note the single hanging scroll, the cha-bana (tea flowers; see p. 184) in the alcove, the patterns in the kimono – each chosen as homage to the seasons and all part of the tearoom meditation.

Tender wagashi (often namagashi – soft, pretty, moulded seasonal sweets) or dry wagashi like wasanbon sugar sweets or kohakutou (see p. 193) are consumed by all before the tea is served, one person at a time, sweetening the palate to mellow the bitterness of the tea. The chawan (tea bowl) is lifted with one hand and given two short turns with the other so that the face or more decorative and interesting side of the bowl is displayed to others in the room. The tea is then consumed in three large sips – ensuring no more than a shadow is left in the bowl, which may be upturned to admire every angle of the craftsperson's work, but not before the face is returned to its original position. At the core of each ceremony is the practice of principals Wa Kei Sei Jaku – translated as harmony, respect, purity and tranquillity.

Eating tips

▶ Make sure Google Translate is set to 'automatic' for restaurant review websites and booking services like Tabelog, Omakase and TableCheck. Most restaurants cannot be booked until two months prior to dining. If a phone call is required, engage your hotel concierge (preferably before you travel!), a friend who speaks Japanese, or just call the venue – sometimes a young employee will speak just enough of your language.

▶ GPS can be interrupted at times, making correctly locating a restaurant difficult if you don't read Japanese characters, so seek other visual cues. Sometimes a noren (split curtain) contains a subtle drawing or symbol advertising the venue's specialty – for example, an eel, chicken, noodles or a bunch of spring onions. Similarly, these may be carved into a wooden plaque or other signage. Noren are also an important check point, reminding you to leave behind the outside world before entering a place where enjoyment and relaxation is the focus.

▶ Some restaurants, particularly in the regions, do not have tables and chairs – so if you can't spend more than an hour sitting on the tatami, it's best to check first. Some restaurants offer horigotatsu as an option – this means that you still sit on the floor, but there's plenty of room for your legs to dangle in a cut-away under a low table.

▶ If you can't read the menu in a casual place, like an izakaya, or aren't sure what to order, say 'osusume' (ohh-sue-sue-meh) 'onegai shimasu' (on-eh-guy she-muss) to the waiter or chef, requesting them to choose for you.

▶ Avoid asking for sauce to come on the side or to swap one item for another on a menu, unless it's a provided option – things don't work like that in Japan. If something is not for you, just eat around it, or gift it to a dining buddy.

▶ It's polite to eat everything (edible) on your plate, so if dietary issues prevent you eating certain things, try to provide advance warning. Ask your hotel concierge, Japanese-speaking friend or a translation app for a note to show at eateries where English is not spoken. Locals are slowly becoming more aware of foreigners' range of intolerances and preferences (even if they don't understand them), but please don't turn up to an okonomiyaki, tempura or katsu restaurant assuming you can order gluten-free on the spot. If you plan ahead, they may be able to accommodate you.

► Be aware that some plate decorations, particularly in kaiseki, are not edible – so if unsure, check before consuming!

► If you're invited to a meeting or formal dining situation, there will be a specific seating order for guests and employees depending on their rank, so running ahead to grab your preferred seat is not an option.

► Likewise, if you are travelling for work and out with Japanese superiors or a VIP, it's traditional to follow their lead when it comes to eating and drinking. To choose something different is to question your superior's tastes, and is therefore disrespectful and a possible cause of embarrassment. This may be a little more relaxed in contemporary business situations with younger creatives, for example. The general rule is to pour drinks for each other, not yourself. Empty glasses will be automatically topped up, so leave yours at least half filled if you are done drinking.

► Request the bill by crossing your two index fingers to make a small X, indicating that proceedings have ended. Note that forearms crossed in an X in front of one's torso means do not enter.

- ▶ Never tip, but do show appreciation by saying 'gochisousama deshita' (gotchy-soh-sah-mah desh-ta) to the chef or server as you leave.

- ▶ If you're lingering in a restaurant after a meal, particularly at the end of kaiseki, a cup of tea lets you know proceedings have ended and you'd best consider making a move. A second cup of tea is a very definite sign you've outstayed your welcome (particularly in Kyoto, or if it's matcha).

- ▶ If the chef or staff come outside to stand by the door and bow you farewell, try not to linger taking photos, which can delay them getting back to work or going home.

- ▶ If you're turned away from a restaurant, please don't automatically attribute the reason to racism as some do. Proprietors who don't speak English sometimes prefer not to cause discomfort to guests or embarrassment to themselves – remember, 'doing your best' is highly important in Japan. Alternatively, they often hold space for loyal regulars, so it may not be as 'empty' as you've perceived. Elderly hosts may simply be overwhelmed by more than a handful of people at a time.

- ▶ If you spot a long queue at an eatery (or another place) it doesn't necessarily mean it's great – sometimes it's the result of group mentality in a heavily populated area, or the result of social media, which likely won't take into account all the equally good (if not better) joints around the corner.

Here's the tea

I've mulled over a selection of graded sen-cha (green tea leaves for infusing); learnt to toast houji-cha (roasted green tea) over a flame; savoured salty kombu-cha (kombu tea – and not what we refer to as 'kombucha' in the West – but that's a connected story worth researching if interested); and sipped ume-cha (dried plum tea) at markets and temples. I've inhaled kyo-bancha (deeply roasted tea) so smoky I had withdrawals; resolved sore throats in winter with sweet ginger or yuzu tea (shoga-cha or yuzu-cha); been obsessed by the nuttiness of both soba-cha and genmai-cha (roasted soba and brown rice teas); quenched thirst on warm days with thermoses of chilled mug-icha (barley tea); become instantly addicted to red shiso tea in the height of summer (made with homemade shiso syrup); and lovingly gazed at the swimming blossoms in sakura tea. Turning to the savoury, I have slurped tea-flavoured noodles and restorative ochazuke (tea over rice). I've experienced several contemporary tea pairings at degustations in fancy restaurants. I have attended cutting-edge tea omakase where tea and tea cocktails were paired with mini wagashi and Western desserts made with Japanese flavours such as azuki (red beans), goma (sesame) and kinako (roasted soybean powder) – you'll find such places popping up in larger cities.

Tea tips

▶ Rooted in Buddhism, publicly available tea-centric affairs are more traditionally practised in areas with more temples, or where imperial or feudal families and associated aristocracy or warriors resided – wherever there were castles or samurai (see p. 175), there were teahouses and geisha. The practice is still very popular in long-time former capital Kyoto, where Buddhism flourished, and also in the ancient capital of Nara. You will find teahouses around castle towns like Kanazawa, or in prominent tea-growing regions (see p. 101/Uji; p. 145/Yame; p. 152/Ureshino; p. 94/Shizuoka and p. 99/Mie). Teahouses or pavilions also feature in many traditional gardens Japan-wide.

▶ Large group ceremonies and tea rituals demonstrated by geisha are occasionally offered to the public during spring festivals.

▶ If you can't sit on the floor during tea ceremony, let your host know beforehand so they can try to arrange some form of seating for you.

▶ Armchair travellers might like to check out Japanese tea ceremony ASMR videos online. Who knew?

▶ There are also now a variety of ways to enjoy and learn about tea in Japan – some of which are highly contemporary. Innovative locals have opened up the tea world in a way that is accessible to foreigners, and in styles that will hopefully attract younger generations of Japanese to engage in tea culture. After all, the ceremony speaks of ultimate hospitality – interpreting guests' needs and level of comfort continue to be an important part of that. Stories must sometimes evolve to remain relevant, if only to encourage interest in their origins.

▶ Shorter, informal tea ceremonies are perfect for novices. Some instructors will talk you through it a first time to loosely explain each action, then allow you to enjoy it again in silence. One of the best businesses I've found for first-timers is operated in Kyoto by

Camellia Tea Ceremony, where you can also request longer and private ceremonies for more detail and education. Takafumi Zenryu Kawakami, head priest of Kyoto's Shunko-in Temple, has on several occasions shared fascinating information on the history and culture of tea ceremony and hospitality from a Zen perspective. If you are interested in Buddhism, zazen meditation and its part in Japanese culture, I highly recommend retreating in the temple's accommodations or enquiring about workshops.

▶ Abbreviated sessions are sometimes operated by ryokan or other accommodations as part of the in-house experience. Hoshinoya in Tokyo, Hachikan Ryokan in Ohara and moksa in Kyoto are some of the first that spring to mind, but do enquire wherever you are staying. I attended a brilliant one-on-one lesson at Maruya Sabou in the Yame tea region's Fukushima village. Perched on a seat inside a simple, tasteful space within the instructor's home, I selected my own chawan and harmonious collection of implements before preparing my matcha. I thoroughly enjoyed asking questions throughout.

▶ You don't have to attend a tea ceremony to enjoy matcha – sometimes service is offered at benches outside tea houses in traditional gardens or villas

(at Okochi Sanso in Kyoto's Arashiyama, tea is included with your entrance ticket). There are also many commercial tea or wagashi salons or shops with tastings or 'tea service' in major cities – simply walk in and order tea and sweets without the formality. Check out Toraya, Higashiya, Kagizen, Suzukake (Fukuoka) and Ippodo Tea (not to be confused with Ippudo's famous ramen store).

▶ Do be aware of koicha – a particularly thick, almost chewy slick of matcha, served as a starter tea in formal ceremonies. Its caffeine kick is stronger than several espressos.

▶ Only purchase matcha in Japan as you are about to leave the country – once it's ground, it only holds its fresh flavour and bright colour for about a month. It's likely sacrilegious, but I store mine in the freezer in hope of prolonging its life – I like to have it on hand for desserts and baked goods.

▶ You can also eat your tea – soft-serve ice cream (sofuto kuriimu) made with quality matcha is sublime. Find the best in tea regions or in traditional cultural precincts. Also keep an eye out for matcha-flavoured chocolate, pudding (purin), cheesecake, ice cream, kakigori (shaved ice with syrup), cookies, roll cakes, candy, cocktails and in salt for tempura.

Above: Hokoku-ji's teahouse, Kamakura.
Below: Cha Cafe Asunaro, Kochi, Shikoku.

Pieces of Japan
– Arts, Crafts and Cultural Entertainments

On a lazy wintery afternoon almost 20 years ago, I found myself lingering in front of a dark timber-and-glass-panelled shopfront in a precinct well known for antiques, vintage wares and traditional items for the home, such as hand-crafted zabuton (flat, square floor cushions); woven, naturally dyed textiles; exquisite incense (see p. 198) and the like. Alone in the store, the shopkeeper beckoned me inside, warmly inviting me to take it easy as I looked around. I hesitated, not sure there was anything I could afford among the beautifully presented wares, but she persuaded me with a kind and genuine smile.

Above: Kumiko woodcraft.
Below: Vintage ceramics at markets.

I noticed that among the array of eye-wateringly expensive items were some incredibly reasonably priced goods, which I later discovered is not uncommon in Japan. No matter how fancy or dowdy a place might look, there can be huge price disparity among the wares, meaning there's treasure for everyone. In other countries, the top-shelf stuff tends to be locked up or closely monitored for theft – for the most part, that's not how Japan works (there are harsh penalties for crime – although, times they are a'changin' and there are possibly more eyes on foreigners now).

Heading for the door, I was drawn to an antique plate. One edge was dipped in an inky-sea glaze – presenting like a film negative of a crescent moon against a time-dulled, sand-hued background. An etched sprig of plum blossom arched towards the crescent, and faintly hand-brushed script languished between. Unable to be seen unless held to the light at a certain angle, a sheer, finely crackled bronze wash wrapped around the plate's entirety.

At around 25,000 yen (about 250 Australian dollars), the price was more than I'd spent on a single plate in my life. Needing further justification for its purchase, I turned to my new friend so neatly presented in her maroon wool skirt, crisp cream shirt and camel-hued cardigan, and asked if she could translate the kanji (script) for me. She explained that the plate was over 200 years old and the script too ancient for her to fully understand, but the essence was, 'In winter and spring you will come.' And there I was, heading into spring, settling into my new home, researching and writing a book about Kyoto's food culture – I couldn't help but suspect this plate was speaking to me. That plate now takes pride of place in my home, where I gaze upon it every day from my writing desk, an ever-present reminder of the importance of openness, connection and chance, and the many stories of the places and people I've encountered in my journey and how they've shaped me.

Traditional arts and crafts

Perched on a purpose-built shelf in the heart of my home (the kitchen, obviously) is a hodgepodge of handmade pottery cups in natural tones from every corner of Japan. Each day, I choose my morning coffee cup to suit my mood or the tone of the day. One that sits snugly in my palms during winter can be strangely soothing. Good friends know to head directly to the shelf before I have a chance to switch on the kettle or espresso machine. It's become a shared, gentle ritual inspired by the Japanese tradition of offering mixed sake cups on a tray, allowing for personal choice; a smile-inducing gesture and excellent icebreaker.

I never leave Japan without a new or pre-loved handmade piece of the country. It could be a found ochoko or recently fired guinomi (small and larger sake cups), a kashigata (antique confectionery mould), an old but unusual sensu (folding fan) or uchiwa (paddle fan) – which I use in summer, or as seasonal décor – or a vintage lacquerware or contemporary ceramic bowl for my table. This could be considered over-consumption, but there's a method to my madness and it speaks of sustainability.

Japan's master shokunin (craftspeople) are at risk. Given today's cost of living in a shiny world that offers too many tempting disposable conveniences, most youth are less interested in kogei – the traditional crafts and applied arts passed down through the generations by their elders. Sometimes we don't know what we have until we lose it. It's difficult to consider a Japan without those who bear the wisdom of monozukuri (objects requiring meticulous skill and knowledge, made with intention and purpose) – and yet, these people are finite in number. To allow the loss or dilution of their knowledge (though it now seems inevitable) would be a travesty – so if you can visit or support just one craftsperson during

your travels, please understand that showing any interest in their wares or skills may play a part in working towards a solution. That is, a greater appreciation for long-lasting, quality, beautiful goods may encourage young Japanese people, who are often influenced by what's popular in the Western world, to reconnect with their own culture and traditions.

In keeping with the Japanese reverence for the seasons, houses have long kept wares like seasonal pottery and tableware, tokonoma scrolls, kimono (or other clothing) and practical furnishings, such as summer's sudare (shade blinds) or mosquito coil burners, in an external storehouse known as kura (originally built to safeguard valuable commodities such as seed, grain and religious artifacts). These homewares are rotated as dictated by the season. Some larger old homes retain this practice – as do many ryokan, ryotei and tasteful kappo-style restaurants – the vessels marrying beautifully with the highly seasonal cuisine.

Above: Making washi at Kamikoya, Yusuhara, Kochi.
Below: Kasuri weaving, Kurume, Fukuoka.

Inspired by this practice, from time to time I'll pack things away at home, bringing out alternative items to replace them – this gives my place a whole new look and energy, even if it's just a few objects. This practice also helps retain their condition, prolonging their existence. In case of vintage and antique wares, this means extending the longevity for things already well loved and utilised. My home is filled with an eclectic collection of quality, long-lasting, practical and decorative, emotive wares, most made from natural materials eons ago in Japan. Truthfully, the enviro-friendly aspect was not my original intention, but I'm delighted by the bonus. And, yes, all of them 'spark joy' – thanks for asking.

The fragments of anything I accidentally break are being saved for kintsugi (golden joinery) repair (take lessons at Poj Studio, Kyoto). This is a grand example of wabi-sabi (see p. 180), as is the bowl my friend fills with age-smoothed pottery shards collected on forest walks throughout Japan, showcasing remnants of history in blue and white. If only these found treasures could speak.

Even before I was aware of the plight of the diminishing shokunin, I'd amassed a range of indigo and other textiles – some from artisans who've passed, their signature patterns never to be repeated. Preserving them felt strangely important, as it did with several pieces of boro (a form of patchwork that repurposes cloth remnants during times of hardship) in compliance with the Japanese philosophy of mottainai (waste not). A kimono in vintage shibori (an intricate form of tie-dye) or that had been heavily embroidered may have taken a year to produce by hand, yet these wearable art pieces can sometimes, shamefully, be picked up for less than the price of a cocktail (although their value is steadily increasing with tourism). And so mottainai does better – wear them, display them on the wall, or turn them into runners or cushions. Just keep the resources circulating.

I'm also mad for old and new noren (split curtains), furoshiki (square cloths for wrapping/carrying – originally a bathhouse tote), tenugui (long cloths used in the kitchen or bathroom, edging purposely unstitched so they dry quickly and deter bacteria) – modern versions of all have been raised to artforms, and are indeed worth framing or using as tablecloths.

Art lovers' highlights and shopping

Aesthetes and art lovers will swoon over the jaw-dropping number of art galleries, museums, outdoor sculpture gardens and design centres throughout the country – too many to attempt to share here. However, you'll easily hash together a starter list from the regional and prefectural mood boards. To help you think outside the box, I also recommend checking out the immersive teamLab experiences, tanbo (rice paddy art), gyotaku (fish prints), fusama

Above: Wood inlay, Hatajuku village, Hakone.
Below: Indigo dyeing, Atelier Yamamura, Fukuoka.

(painted sliding door art best seen in preserved traditional buildings with strong cultural relevance) and even Tokyo's toilet project. See what else you can flush out in your online search. If contemporary art festivals float your boat, you'll want to know about the art triennales of the Setouchi, Aichi, Echigo-Tsumari and Oku-noto regions.

If you are hunting down classic art pieces for home – think mokuhanga (woodblock prints, famously Ukiyoe and Hokusai), netsuke (small carvings, originally ivory) or Noh masks – you'll find them at specialist art and craft stores, like Kyoto Handicraft Center, department stores, markets and sometimes around tourist precincts. Flea market books can be excellent sources of traditional Japanese imagery and illustration worth framing.

Kokeshi dolls are popular souvenirs, though the origin of these items is unclear. One rumour suggests that in ancient times, when food was scarce, male children were preferred in sustaining farming

Kokeshi dolls and other flea and antique market spoils.

communities, and therefore unwanted female babies were strangled with vines and abandoned. It's said that to appease the baby's spirit, kokeshi were carved in their honour and painted with the vine or plant used in their demise. Online there are various theories, variations and debunkings. Without ancient records, we'll never know for certain. Dark tourism fodder, for sure.

While I no longer seek out kokeshi, I house a growing community of regional Daruma dolls. Modelled on the tenacious Bodhidharma (the founder of Zen Buddhism), Daruma dolls are representative of the commitment and perseverance so valued in Japan, and you'll see his likeness everywhere. Commonly painted protective red and rounded in shape (limbless), they are not without variation in the regions, bearing the marks of local craftspeople and their communities. Luck is a constant theme in Japan, and I recommend reading up on the legends around the Darumas' extremities (and eyelids). Small Daruma, made from papier-mâché, come without pupils – you paint one in when wishing for success in a project or concept and the other once it's been realised. In gratitude, you let go of him in a special temple bonfire at Setsubun (see p. 174), making way for new endeavours.

My husband will have you know he does not collect 'dollies' (as I refer to them), but figures. From action to anime characters, these collectibles are super popular. While precincts like Akihabara or Nakano in Tokyo are well known, there are second-hand or 'recycle/upcycle' stores all around the country.

If you're into folk art, don't miss Kyoto's Kawai Kanjiro House or Tokyo's Mingei International Museum and similar (which can be well tucked away in the regions), showcasing true local style and form.

Performing arts

Of course, Japan's performing arts are utterly mesmerising and include kabuki and Noh (both classic musical dramas including dance, costumes and stories). Nihon-buyoh (traditional Japanese dance) is sometimes performed by geisha at small dance theatres (kaburenjo) located in geisha districts known as a hanamachi (flower towns). Butoh (avant-garde dance and movement), rakugo (storytelling), kyogen (comedy), bunraku (puppetry), odori (folk dance and music) can all be enjoyed at event and performance spaces or specially purposed theatres. Musical performances in classic court form (gagaku) or folk style can be a single-instrument affair or a combined effort incorporating shakuhachi and shinobue (flutes), shamisen (similar to a banjo), Okinawan sanshin (a larger shamisen), biwa (lute), koto (longboard zither), taiko (drumming) and so on. Look for advertised – sometimes free – performances on local tourism or community sites and book tickets ahead if you can.

> ✽ Due to the influx of tourism in certain districts and the behaviour by certain disrespectful travellers (I've seen people grab geisha to pull them in for a snap), it's now very difficult to receive permission for photography. However, if there's no-one else about, you might like to gently approach with a 'sumimasen' and an apologetic smile – furtively holding your camera in sight, and asking 'shashin wa' (sha-shin-wah), 'daijoubu desu ka?' (dye-jaw-bu-desk-a) – meaning 'is a photo okay?' Do not persist if they keep on moving.

Regional folk music (min'yo), often observed at outdoor festivals, can be infectiously lively – some hotels and ryokan (such as those operated by Hoshino Resorts) may offer it as free in-house entertainment. Listening to magical shomyo (monks chanting) at

temples is otherworldly, and enka's sentimental ballads can be heard at oldschool karaoke cafes and bars.

Of course, there are incredible music festivals around the country, from oldschool jazz to the latest J-pop. If that scene feels too crowded or loud for you, listening bars may offer solace.

We should not forget martial arts like sumo (wrestling), karate (empty-hand fighting), judo (throws and holds), kendo (swords), aikido (defensive grappling), kyudo (archery) and many other lesser-known disciplines. Some offer pay-to-view performances, and if you're lucky you'll stumble across a demonstration at a special cultural day or event. Some schools will allow viewing with special permission. Elsewhere, you'll find private lessons.

Perhaps it's in their DNA, but the Japanese view or sense things in ways that are sometimes unfamiliar to us. Maybe this explains why their arts and cultural entertainments are so damn enthralling. There's much to see.

Above: Traditional Ryukyu folk music and dance, Okinawa.
Below: Avant-garde Butoh.

Tips for seeing Japanese arts, crafts and culture

▶ You'll find a range of regional arts and crafts information listed throughout the regional and prefectural mood boards, but you will discover far more in situ. The deeper you travel regionally, the more you'll be exposed to.

▶ Join an arts or craft-related tour or hire an expert guide to escort or assist you visiting craftspeople for a deeper understanding. Maybe you'd like to explore the history and wares of the six most noteworthy ancient pottery kilns of Japan and beyond advised by an expert like Robert Yellin of Yakimono Gallery (pottery wares), or someone who can introduce you to makers of everything from hand-carved kashigata (wagashi mould) or Noh masks. It's an investment worth making.

▶ Upskill – there are many starter ideas for classes or workshops above or in the prefectural mood boards. You might also consider forging your own blade, pinching a pot, making washi paper, assembling a kite or fan or creating your own incense blend. Paint a maneki-neko, learn to trim a bonsai, repair something of importance with kintsugi, try your hand at shodo (calligraphy), sumi-e (ink painting), shikki (lacquerware) or puzzle together wood kumiko (latticework). Weave a bamboo basket or textile piece, stitch cloth with sashiko, dye your own indigo shibori apparel or hammer a metal saucepan. Create realistic wax food models (like those in restaurant windows) or model miniatures like Japanese foods, dioramas or figurines.

▶ Seek out tezukuri-ichi (handmade markets), design, flea and antique markets – you'll find some recommendations throughout this book.

▶ You'll find handcrafted kitchen- and tablewares in various venues including department stores, food markets, specialist knife stores and in kitchen towns such as Kappabashi in Tokyo or Osaka's Sennichimae Doguyasuji.

▶ If you're seriously taken with a particular traditional craft (such as the real indigo dyeing – not the chemical garbage used so freely around the

world today), check out Japanese villages known for growing the indigo plant or producing wares (aizome). In the case of indigo dyeing, you could try Fukuoka's Kurume, Tokushima's Wakimachi, Nagoya's Arimatsu or Okayama's Kojima (the birthplace of Japanese denim).

▶ Before you buy traditional arts and crafts, make sure you get what you pay for. If a cast iron teapot seems strangely cheaper than you've seen elsewhere, it may have been made offshore from inferior quality materials. For authentic products, seek out the shokunin, as mentioned above, even if you buy them after returning home through reputable companies like Shokunin Store (shokuninstore.com), who will ship to you.

▶ If the scent (kaori) of quality incense (koh) appeals for home, you'll find an immaculate selection sold at temple or shrine adjacent stores or famous independent stores like Kungyokudo (the oldest incense store in Japan), Shoyeido (established in Kyoto in the 1700s) or their offshoot Lisn for something fresh and contemporary. Sachets of soothing, aromatic powdered incense can deodorise your wardrobe, handbag or car. Delectable essential oils focused on Japanese flowers, wood oils like hinoki (cypress) or citrus like yuzu are also easy to find, but be sure to look out for Japanese perfumes paying homage to Japan's florals. I am particularly fond of the brand J-Scent, but there are others – often very local potions you won't find elsewhere.

Pottery wares from from Okinawa (top) and Karatsu, Kyushu.

Good to Know (GTK)

– Essentials, Etiquette and Useful Extras (or, how not to be an f-wit tourist in Japan)

While the idea of winging an entire Japan journey appeals to me on some level, I am equally fond of certain creature comforts, like a supportive mattress. I can only sleep on futon-topped tatami for one or two nights before I need to seek the 'bone doctor' for spinal realignment. There are a few things in Japan that are better *not* left to the universe, unless you are extremely flexible with your time, schedule (and body), and/or bottomless credit.

Acquaint yourself with local customs before you travel.

DOCUMENTATION

Passports – it's required that you always carry them. You may be stopped and asked to produce yours.

Insurance, visas (if required), international driver's licences (if hiring a car) and a copy of medical scripts and/or a letter from your doctor listing your medication needs may also be crucial (see medication below).

SAFETY FIRST

Japan is not an overtly safe theme park, as many seem to believe, although it's certainly less risky than most other countries. Fortunately, travellers are highly unlikely to be affected by organised crime and for the most part opportunistic incidents are likely to cause only minor discomfort, embarrassment or inconvenience – but it pays to be aware. Anyone identifying as female should take precaution later in the evenings, such as using 'women only' train carriages when they are available. Those stories about people leaving their laptop or handbag on the train only to have it returned the next day are true – but occasional theft, like shoplifting, is said to be on the rise.

GUIDES

A private guide or translator can make or break your trip, so it's well worth seeking a personal recommendation. While accredited guides are trained and knowledgeable, it can sometimes sound like they are reading from a script. Unless they've lived or travelled extensively overseas, I've found that many Japanese guides don't understand what international tourists are looking for and are unable to improvise or adapt as necessary – but a good one is pure gold.

Japan Federation of Certified Guides (jfg-e.jp) is an excellent resource, as is GoWithGuide (gowithguide.com/japan) (which has reviews) to find guides who either reside or specialise in your areas of interest – this could be regions (try local tourism links too), but also topics (such as architecture, history, nature or food). However, availability or responses are not always guaranteed, so start your hunt early.

There are also volunteer guides (which I imagine can be hit or miss – sometimes you get what you pay for). Some taxi drivers also offer a drive/guide service, and I hear (but cannot confirm) that some university students are happy to act as a guide or translator in exchange for a decent feed or drinks.

ACCOMMODATION

When Japan reopened post-pandemic, inbound tourism superseded the already surging pre-COVID crush. Accommodation became one essential worth pencilling in – particularly in better known cities or ski regions in season – at least for the first few days, even when 'wandering where your heart takes you' for an extended period. Japanese hotels have leapt up in price since COVID, and prices can also surge with demand the closer it gets to your stay.

FYI, although things are slowly changing, many hotels in regional areas do not have king or queen beds – instead, you usually find twins (two single beds), and they can't always be pushed together due to secured cabinetry in-between. Also check for shared bathrooms, if that's something you'd rather avoid.

If you're staying at accommodation with onsen, don't assume you can use them if you have tattoos, which are associated with organised crime in Japan. Cover them up unless you've been given the green light or access to private onsen use.

Recommendations

Upmarket/Special

- **Tokyo** – Aman Tokyo, Andaz, Grand Hyatt, Hyatt Regency, Hoshinoya Tokyo, Hotel Toranomon Hills, Imperial Hotel, Mandarin Oriental, Park Hyatt, The Lively Tokyo Azabujuban, The Okura, The Prince Park Tower, The Ritz-Carlton, The Strings by InterContinental, The Tokyo Station Hotel.
- **Kanagawa** – Hoshino Resorts Kai Sengokuhara.
- **Kyoto (and Kansai)** – Ace Hotel, Aman Kyoto, Banyan Tree Higashiyama, Fauchon Hotel, Garrya, Good Nature Hotel, Hachikan Ryokan (Ohara), Hanase Highland Inn (Hanase), Hoshinoya Kyoto, Hotel Higashiyama Tokyu, Hotel Seiryu, Hyatt Regency, Imperial Hotel Kyoto, Kyoto Machiya Stays, Machiya Residence Inn, moksa, Nohga Hotel Kiyomizu, Roku Kyoto, The Brighton Hotel, The Hiramatsu, The Okura Kyoto Bettei, The Square, The Ritz-Carlton Kyoto, Shima Kanko Hotel the Classic (Mie), Fufu Nara, Noborioji Hotel Nara, Sasayuri-Ann (Uda, Nara).
- **Fukuoka** – Craft inn Te (Yame), Harazuku no Mai (Ukiha), Hilltop Resort, Seiryuan Ryokan (Akizuki), Tachibana-tei Ohana (Yanagawa), The Royal Park Canvas Fukuoka Nakasu.
- **Aichi** – Nikko Style Nagoya, Indigo Hotel Inuyama.
- **Aomori** – Kai Tsugaru.
- **Ishikawa** – Hyatt Centric, Kai Kaga (Kaga Onsen), Machiya Residence Inn, Sainoniwa Hotel, Uan (Kanazawa), Flatts (Noto).
- **Karatsu** – Oncri Karatsu.
- **Kochi** – Auberge Tosayama.
- **Kurashiki** – Ryokan Kurashiki.
- **Nagano** – Hotel Shoho Matsumoto.
- **Naoshima** – Ryokan Roka, The Benesse House.
- **Niigata** – AIR Myoko.
- **Tochigi** – The Ritz-Carlton Nikko, Kai Nikko, Kai Kinugawa.

- **Okinawa** – Hoshinoya Taketomi Island, Hyatt Regency Naha and Seragaki Island, The Terrace Club at Busena.
- **Ozu** – Nipponia Hotel.
- **Shizuoka** – ABBA Resorts Izu.
- **Yamaguchi** – Hoshino Resorts Kai Nagato.
- **Yusuhara** – Kumo no Ueno Hotel Annex.

More affordable
Comfortable hotel groups or chains:

Agora, The Blossom, Candeo, Fairfield Inn by Marriott, Hagi no Yado Tomoe, Hoshino Resorts OMO brand (OMO3, 5 or 7 – the higher the number, the more facilities), JR Hotel Clement, Apartment Hotel Mimaru, Mitsui Garden Hotels, Resol Hotels, Richmond Hotels, Royal Park Hotels, Tokyu Stays.

Alternatives
Hosted home or farmstays. There's no central booking system, but some can be booked via regional portals by searching for 'noka minpaku' (green tourism), homestays or farmstays in your area of interest. They can sometimes be found on Airbnb, Booking.com, Rakuten Travel or similar.

Temple or castle stays. Airbnb homes and apartments. Ski lodges, camping, glamping, caravans, motor homes, riverside treehouse cabins and ice hotels. Floating hotels or overnight cruising. Upmarket hostels or capsule hotels (very affordable options, unsuited to claustrophobics or those of above-average height/weight). Themed or character hotels. Love hotels – by the hour ;) but they can make for an affordable overnight stay.

Hachikan Ryokan, Ohara.

Etiquette

▶ Hugging – don't do it unless a Japanese person initiates it. Sometimes when working or socialising with a foreigner, a modern-thinking Japanese person may instigate a hug – to make *you* feel more comfortable.

▶ Bowing – not only do people bow instead of shaking hands, but the depth of the bow is indicative of hierarchy and respect. To bow too low or too high can be perceived as sarcasm or rudeness. Watch those beside you and follow their lead if possible. However, as a foreigner, you will be forgiven for screwing it up.

▶ Perfume, cologne and aftershave – avoid wearing it on public transport (or in other confined spaces), in restaurants or food production facilities (like sake breweries).

▶ Smoking – while larger cities are banning smoking outdoors in certain precincts and special smoking rooms with strong exhausts are installed in many buildings (like airports and hotels), there are still restaurants and bars, particularly in the countryside, where people smoke openly inside. If it worries you, it's probably best to have a quick sniff before you sit down.

- ▶ Noise – avoid talking loudly or at all on the bus or commuter train, and do not make or take phone calls (unless it's a real emergency, then put your phone on silent), or play games or music unless you have headphones on.

- ▶ Dining – basic chopstick etiquette can make the difference between a lovely meal and one filled with silent insults. The oshibori (wet towels) are for using before and sometimes during your meal. Don't wipe it over your face or neck; simply wipe your hands clean and then fold neatly. You can dab sticky fingers on it during your meal if necessary. In fancy joints, you'll receive a second before sweets and tea.

- ▶ Stand back – taxi doors are automatically opened by the driver. Don't be tempted to open them when hopping out, unless you are in the front seat, which should only occur if there are three or more passengers.

- ▶ Use discretion when blowing your nose or sneezing. Neither are viewed as polite to do in public, so take it to the bathroom or around a corner if you can, or simply turn away.

- ▶ Shopping – when you buy something at a supermarket, the cashier will ask you if you need a bag (fukuro), which are paid for to reduce waste. Hold up as many fingers as you think you'll need. Better still, carry eco bags when shopping. On the flipside, when you buy food in a department store, you may be appalled at the amount of packaging. The amount of paper and plastic utilised in Japan can be daunting at first. As beautiful and purposeful as it is, it does feel wasteful, but the country is making ground-breaking progress in biodegradable, eco-safe 'plastic' packaging made from rice, seaweed or other plant-based materials. You'll likely be asked how many hours until you are home so they can make sure your cream cake has enough dry ice to keep it cold until you arrive at your accommodation.

- ▶ Try to give exact change wherever you can – like in shops, restaurants and taxis. Place it on the small tray provided. Do not hand money directly to your server.

COMMUNICATION

If always being contactable or being connected to wi-fi is important to you, buy an eSIM before you travel or hire a portable wi-fi unit – try Sakura Mobile (sakuramobile.jp) or Global Advanced Communications (globaladvancedcomm.com), who deliver to your hotel or arrival airport and are reliable. If you are travelling with a group, note that some units allow up to a dozen people to connect, saving on cost. Of course, that only works when you're all together.

PHOTOGRAPHY

Japan is a photographer's paradise, but remember to be considerate of those around you. Sometimes there can be many people trying to get the same shot. Be patient, and ideally ask permission to publish, even on social media, if there's a subject or a business involved that is clearly recognisable. Don't use flash in restaurants or galleries. Remember that some places won't let you take photos at all, so check first.

If in doubt, take the lead of locals around you – observe their actions and copy them.

GIFTS

Do take small, attractively wrapped gifts (presentation is important) in case you meet or visit with someone, or a person is particularly helpful or kind. Ideally, it should be something connected to your own country, and if it's food or drink it shows consideration for not dumping them with something that takes up valuable room in compact living spaces. Present gifts towards the end of proceedings, not as soon as you get there.

CLOTHING

Pack for Japan's four distinctive seasons (see p. 172). Most importantly, take good walking shoes. Dress comfortably but neatly for everyday travel, but feel free to dress up for important occasions and meetings, or upmarket restaurants – this is more relevant in larger cities. Regional areas are far more casual.

TRANSPORT

Major airports in Japan have a range of transport options into the city you're staying – trains, buses, private transfers and more. If you're considering taxis, know that Narita International Airport in Tokyo and KIX in Kansai are quite a distance from Tokyo and Kyoto cities, compared with Haneda Airport (Tokyo) and Itami Airport (Kansai). You can easily take a taxi from Haneda to your city hotel, but attempting that from Narita costs a bomb. From Narita, I prefer to take a limousine bus (direct to hotel) or Narita Express Train (quicker, but you then need to jump on a local line, bus or taxi from the station), or a private set-price transfer – door-to-door.

Japan Rail Passes (for use on JR Railways) used to be an absolute bargain, but prices have increased in recent times – so much so that unless you are travelling far and wide over consecutive days (passes come in 7-, 14- or 21-day deals), on Japan Railways-owned lines only, it may be more cost effective to buy separate tickets.

It is convenient to have the pass, but you can also consider buying PASMO, Suica, ICOCA or similar 'top up, tap and go' cards as needed.

A wide variety of commuter lines also offer additional premium, sometimes themed, sightseeing day trip trains. These boast wide windows, comfy furnishings, limited stops, food service, cultural aspects, live music and more. Do a simple online search like 'what special/luxury/themed trains travel to ...' (insert your desired destination) and you'll be surprised with what pops up – options include the Premium Express Shimakaze (Mie), SPACIA X (Nikko) and The Seven Stars (Kyushu). There are also seasonal and vintage train rides like Aomori's snow shovel trains, which plough through the snow while you're savouring grilled squid snacks and sake!

DRIVING

Unless you're a skilled, confident driver, save this for less busy regions with simple routes and traffic-free roads – think Kyushu, Hokkaido (outside of winter) and Okinawa – or most places distanced from larger cities. However, no matter where you go, mountainous or hilly areas can be riddled with challenging goat tracks suited to small vehicles only, so try to stick to main roads where you can.

LUGGAGE

Taking a large suitcase on the Shinksansen (or other long-distance trains) is not advised. There may be a carriage with lockable storage if you're lucky or, if you book early, you might score that one seat at either end of the carriage with more legroom, or pay for an equally rare oversized luggage seat. Otherwise, it's just an overhead rack, made for smaller bags – larger cases may be removed, so don't risk it.

Luggage forwarding services are a better option and offer safe and reliable door-to-door transport of large suitcases and parcels, which take one or two days to arrive, depending how far they are travelling. Enquire about Takkyubin/Takuhaibin/Yamato transport (aka 'Kuroneko', for the company logo's signature black cats) at your hotel, airport, convenience store or main train stations or ferry terminals – some also have lockers for short-term storage. Then simply travel with an overnight bag and essential medicines and valuables, etc.

PERSONAL

Toilets

Luxe Japanese toilets with bells and whistles might be the subject of dinner party conversation around the globe, but public toilets aren't always easy to locate in Japan. Of course, in cities there are all the usual fail-safes like department stores and large fast food or coffee joints. However, it's handy to know that, while it's not advertised, there's usually a single toilet at the back of convenience stores – excellent when you're desperate. While some people simply walk out when they're done, I like to show my appreciation by buying something small as I'm leaving.

Medical

Japanese pharmacists usually speak a little English and can be helpful for many basic ailments.

If you need remote medical advice in English, 24/7 assistance is available online via MediConnect (english.mediconnectjapan.com).

TELL Japan is a toll-free, English-speaking line for mental health support. You can call them on 0800–300–8355.

Emergency numbers worth knowing are for ambulance and fire (119), and police (110).

In an emergency, visiting hospitals or specialised clinics (ENT, for example) in large cities can be very streamlined and efficient with the latest, top-of-the-line technology. Some English is usually spoken in cities but not always in the countryside. Travel insurance is essential.

Useful phrases:

I'm sick – Byoki desu (byawky dess)

Help! – Tasukete (tuss-kehteh)

Hospital – Byoin (byaw-inn)

Ambulance – Kyuukyuusha (queue-queue-shah)

Hospital emergency – Kyukyuu shochishitsu (queue-queue shochi-shitzu)

Medication
Check Japan travel advisories or the Japanese Embassy in your country to confirm which medications you can and can't travel with or that may need special documentation. Japan has strict laws around certain drugs (even some prescription medications for ADHD or similar) and heavy fines or punishments are observed. Cannabis may be legal in your country, but it's not in Japan. Breaking any law in Japan (especially if it's drug-related) can attract very harsh penalties, so if you're unsure, ask.

Alternative therapies
I recommend looking into shiatsu (wear loose clothing for this 'dry' massage), hari (acupuncture), reiki (energy healing), moxibustion (burning mugwort to heat points in the body, stimulating qi and blood flow), kampo (herbal medicine), zazen (meditation), kobido (non-invasive face lift massage).

You'll also find a range of clean, reputable and easy-to-book (some online) massage and reflexology shops around train stations or busy shopping areas. Your feet will thank you.

Onsen, containing a variety of minerals, are popular for relaxing, healing (skin, joints and muscles) and general health. Some have higher temperatures than others, so check before you enter, especially if you have uncontrolled high blood pressure. Tattoos are banned in most onsens.

Further Reading/Viewing

Recommendations for several books, websites and other forms of published information are scattered throughout the previous pages. Here are a few others I recommend:

BOOKS AND MANGA

Kitchen by Banana Yoshimoto – just one of her colourful, quirky novels – I've long been a fan of her work.

The Pillow Book by Sei Shonagon – a fascinating glimpse into Japanese court life of the 11th century.

Snow Country by Yasunari Kawabata – captures the essence of old Japan in winter.

Sushi and Beyond by Michael Booth – a fun and easy foodie read.

Tokyo Vice by Jake Adelstein – a journalist takes a thrilling peek into Japan's organised crime (now also a streaming series).

Anything written by Haruki Murakami is hugely popular – *Norwegian Wood* and *Kafka on the Shore* are among his best-known – although I confess to not having finished any of his recent works.

The collectible culinary-manga series *Oishinbo* is gold for foodie otaku (nerds) passionate about Japanese cuisine. Ahem ...

I've not read *Shogun* by James Clavell, but enjoyed the recent streaming series,

which I recommend as an entry point into Japan's feudal history. It shows how warfare and social order influenced today's Japanese society and culture.

When in Japan, go play at any Tsutaya, Kinokuniya or Maruzen/Junkudo bookstore, as they have a tonne of fabulous books, magazines and mooks on Japanese culture, design, food and often great gift sections too.

FILMS AND TV SERIES

Departures (Okuribito) (2008) – an exquisite, very human story centred on Japan's funeral culture.

Lost in Translation (2003) – the only movie I've watched on repeat. It reminds me of my Tokyo life during the affluent 80s 'bubble period', so called for its inflated economy.

The Makanai (2023, streaming) – a charming series about geiko and maiko life in Kyoto.

Midnight Diner (2009, streaming) – a fly-on-the-wall look at the guests of a late-night eatery.

Perfect Days (2023) – directed by Wim Wenders, co-written with Takuma Takasaki. The film follows the routine life of Hirayama (Koji Yakusho) – a public toilet cleaner in Tokyo – but speaks of so much more.

Sunny (2024, streaming) – a quirky dramedy about a woman and her robot, mainly shot in Kyoto.

Tampopo (1985) – an absolute must-watch for foodies; a cult 'ramen Western' with great insight into Japanese lifestyle and curiosities.

A Taxing Woman (1987) and *A Taxing Woman's Return* (1988) – sharp Japanese comedies from the 1980s.

Tokyo Story (1953) – a cinematic classic about post-war generational divide and aging in Japan.

Keep an eye out for the Japan Film Festival (JFF), which tours internationally through Japan Foundation offices and partner cinemas in various countries.

Also, you could check out Studio Ghibli classics like *My Neighbour Totoro* (1988) and *Spirited Away* (2001), if you haven't already. Hayao Miyazaki's beautiful animation provides fascinating takes on the supernatural, nature and friendship.

ONLINE

It would have taken four more decades to write this book without the support of a few Japan tourism legends: Alison Roberts Brown of Tourism Garden (tourismgarden.com.au), the teams at Kyokanko/Kyoto City Official Guide (kyoto.travel/en), TCVB/Go Tokyo (gotokyo.org), JAMS.TV, The DOQ, JTB, JETRO, JNTO, and Rebecca George (SLC Australia). Do seek out their websites or helpful newsletters!

Also check out local publications such as Kyoto Journal (kyotojournal.org), Kyoto visitors guide (kvg-kyoto.com), Time Out city guides (timeout.com/japan), the Japan Times (japantimes.co.jp), Metropolis (metropolisjapan.com), Tokyo Weekender (tokyoweekender.com), anything by writers/podcasters Amy Chavez (*Books on Asia*), Lee Tran Lam (@leetranlam) or Florentyna Leow (@furochan_eats).

Websites and blogs on specific personal interests written by foreign or Japanese individuals who openly share their own experiences, insight and tips are also worth trawling for. If it's not in English, simply use an online translation app like Google Translate.

LOCAL TOURISM WEBSITES

Hokkaido	visit-hokkaido.jp/en
Aomori	aomori-tourism.com/en
Iwate	iwatetabi.jp/en
Miyagi	visitmiyagi.com
Akita	stayakita.com
Yamagata	yamagatakanko.com/en
Fukushima	fukushima.travel
Ibaraki	visit.ibarakiguide.jp/en
Tochigi	visit-tochigi.com
Gunma	visit-gunma.jp/en
Saitama	saitama-supportdesk.com
Chiba	visitchiba.jp

Tokyo	gotokyo.org/en
Kanagawa	trip.pref.kanagawa.jp
Niigata	enjoyniigata.com/en
Toyama	visit-toyama-japan.com/en
Ishikawa	ishikawatravel.jp/en
Fukui	fuku-e.com/en
Yamanashi	yamanashi-kankou.jp/english
Nagano	go-nagano.net/en
Gifu	visitgifu.com
Shizuoka	exploreshizuoka.jp/en
Aichi	aichinow.pref.aichi.jp/en
Mie	visitmie-japan.travel/en
Shiga	en.biwako-visitors.jp
Kyoto	kyototourism.org/en
Osaka	osaka-info.jp
Hyogo	hyogo-tourism.jp/world
Nara	visitnara.jp
Wakayama	visitwakayama.jp/en
Tottori	tottori-tour.jp/en
Shimane	kankou-shimane.com/en
Okayama	okayama-japan.jp/en
Hiroshima	dive-hiroshima.com/en
Yamaguchi	visit-jy.com/en
Tokushima	discovertokushima.net/en
Kagawa	my-kagawa.jp/en
Ehime	visitehimejapan.com/en
Kochi	visitkochijapan.com/en
Fukuoka	crossroadfukuoka.jp/en
Saga	asobo-saga.jp/en
Nagasaki	discover-nagasaki.com/en
Kumamoto	kumamoto.guide/en
Oita	oita-tourism.com/en
Miyazaki	kanko-miyazaki.jp/en
Kagoshima	kagoshima-kankou.com/for
Okinawa	visitokinawajapan.com

Acknowledgements

To Pip Williams – thanks for introducing me to the incredible team at Affirm Press who 'got it' straight away and generously allowed me to dance around in this project for longer than ideal, when life unexpectedly interrupted ...

To the editors who reined in my word count when it turned encyclopaedic and the designers who added texture and life to the pages.

Arigatou Ruby Ashby Orr, Kevin O'Brien and team for your trust, flexibility and collaboration.

With enormous love and gratitude to: my amazing mum, Anne, for her endless support; my patient, tenacious brother, Adam, and his gorgeous offspring; my loving, brilliant, brave, and effing funny husband, Gerard; and to our fur-baby, Yuki-chan, who makes even the darkest day bright.

To dear family and dear friends who left this crazy planet during the last 18 months – you are ever loved and missed: Barnes, Eva, Lorraine and Maxie. And to those of you still present in the flesh, thank you – for listening, sharing, encouraging, understanding, inspiring and being kind. Too many of you to name – but you know who you are.

Travel well and deeply. Jane x